CAMBRIDGE LIBRARY COLLECTION

Books of enduring scholarly value

History

The books reissued in this series include accounts of historical events and movements by eye-witnesses and contemporaries, as well as landmark studies that assembled significant source materials or developed new historiographical methods. The series includes work in social, political and military history on a wide range of periods and regions, giving modern scholars ready access to influential publications of the past.

The Verses Formerly Inscribed on Twelve Windows in the Choir of Canterbury Cathedral

M.R. James (1862–1936) is probably best remembered as a writer of chilling ghost stories, but he was an outstanding scholar of medieval literature and palaeography, who served both as Provost of King's College, Cambridge, and as Director of the Fitzwilliam Museum. His short book from 1901 on the texts inscribed in the famous stained-glass windows of Canterbury Cathedral is paired here with an anonymous guide to the windows published in 1897. Its author is believed to have been Emily Williams, whose aim was 'to give some account of the changes which have taken place in the arrangement of the old painted glass' during the major restoration which was taking place throughout the nineteenth century. The preface is by Dean Farrar, the author of the popular morality tale for children, *Eric, or Little by Little*, and all proceeds were to go to the Cathedral Restoration Fund.

T0382121

Cambridge University Press has long been a pioneer in the reissuing of out-of-print titles from its own backlist, producing digital reprints of books that are still sought after by scholars and students but could not be reprinted economically using traditional technology. The Cambridge Library Collection extends this activity to a wider range of books which are still of importance to researchers and professionals, either for the source material they contain, or as landmarks in the history of their academic discipline.

Drawing from the world-renowned collections in the Cambridge University Library, and guided by the advice of experts in each subject area, Cambridge University Press is using state-of-the-art scanning machines in its own Printing House to capture the content of each book selected for inclusion. The files are processed to give a consistently clear, crisp image, and the books finished to the high quality standard for which the Press is recognised around the world. The latest print-on-demand technology ensures that the books will remain available indefinitely, and that orders for single or multiple copies can quickly be supplied.

The Cambridge Library Collection will bring back to life books of enduring scholarly value (including out-of-copyright works originally issued by other publishers) across a wide range of disciplines in the humanities and social sciences and in science and technology.

The Verses Formerly Inscribed on Twelve Windows in the Choir of Canterbury Cathedral

Together with Notes on the Painted Glass of Canterbury Cathedral

MONTAGUE RHODES JAMES
EMILY WILLIAMS

CAMBRIDGE
UNIVERSITY PRESS

CAMBRIDGE UNIVERSITY PRESS

Cambridge, New York, Melbourne, Madrid, Cape Town, Singapore,
São Paolo, Delhi, Dubai, Tokyo

Published in the United States of America by Cambridge University Press, New York

www.cambridge.org
Information on this title: www.cambridge.org/9781108011334

This edition first published 1901
This digitally printed version 2010

ISBN 978-1-108-01133-4 Paperback

THE VERSES FORMERLY INSCRIBED ON

TWELVE WINDOWS

IN THE CHOIR OF

CANTERBURY CATHEDRAL.

PUBLICATIONS: OCTAVO SERIES

No. XXXVIII

THE VERSES FORMERLY INSCRIBED ON

TWELVE WINDOWS

IN THE CHOIR OF

CANTERBURY CATHEDRAL.

REPRINTED, FROM THE MANUSCRIPT, WITH INTRODUCTION AND NOTES

BY

MONTAGUE RHODES JAMES, Litt.D..

FELLOW AND TUTOR OF KING'S COLLEGE, CAMBRIDGE.
DIRECTOR OF THE FITZWILLIAM MUSEUM.

Cambridge :

PRINTED FOR THE CAMBRIDGE ANTIQUARIAN SOCIETY.

SOLD BY DEIGHTON, BELL & CO.; AND MACMILLAN & BOWES.

LONDON, GEORGE BELL AND SONS.

1901

PREFATORY NOTE.

I HOPE to follow up the present tract by editions of other iconographical texts of less meagre proportions. Foremost among these I contemplate issuing the text of the book called *Pictor in Carmine*, to which many allusions are made in the accompanying pages. I will here subjoin a list of the manuscripts of this work which are at present known to me, partly for the convenience of students, and partly in the hope that other copies may be recognised. The first words of the table of subjects are: "Colloquium Gabrielis et Virginis." The Prologue begins: "Dolens in sanctuario dei." I shall be very grateful for any additions to my list of authorities.

1. Corpus Christi College, Cambridge, no. 217. An incomplete text from Worcester.

2. *Ibid.*, no. 300. A fine manuscript, which contains only *Pictor*. I have a complete transcript of it.

3. Bodl. Rawlinson A. 425. Containing only *Pictor*. Imperfect at the end.

4. Bodl. Digby 65, ff. 79—102.

5. Durham, Bp. Cosin's Library V. II. 5.

6. Phillipps, 11059. Sir Thomas Phillipps printed the Prologue from this MS. in one of his Catalogues, and M. Delisle has reprinted it in *Mélanges de Paléographie*, etc., p. 205.

Two other remarks may be made in this place. Firstly, the term "Theological," as applied to windows containing pictures of types and antitypes, is borrowed ultimately, I believe, from the works of MM. Cahier and Martin. I derive it directly from Mr Westlake's *History of Design in Painted Glass*. Secondly, the punctuation of the verses printed in the tract is that supplied by the manuscript; I do not wish any readers to hold me responsible for it. They must punctuate for themselves if they desire to get any sense out of the lines.

M. R. J.

THE TWELVE THEOLOGICAL WINDOWS

OF

CANTERBURY CATHEDRAL.

THE SOURCE OF THE VERSES.

The verses inscribed upon certain painted windows in Canterbury Cathedral have been printed more than once. First by W. Somner in his *Antiquities of Canterbury*, 1640: then by Battely in his edition of Somner in 1703: again in Winston's *Hints on Stained Glass*, from Somner's text: most recently in an admirable little book written by a lady (who remains anonymous), and issued with a preface by the present Dean of Canterbury in 1897 under the title of *Notes on the Painted Glass in Canterbury Cathedral*. I wish to do what I can to call attention to this work: it seems to me exactly what is wanted. I should very much like to see books on the same plan done for York and for others of our churches which possess considerable remains of ancient glass. That is by the way: I was about to say that the text of the verses in this book was taken from a seventeenth century transcript by Brian Twyne in MS. 256, at Corpus Christi College, Oxford.

So far as I can gather, none of the editors since Battely's time have consulted the oldest MS. authority available: and since the verses are particularly interesting, and the text as hitherto printed sometimes obscure, I have thought it well to consult the original document from which Somner took them. The Dean and Chapter of Canterbury Cathedral most generously lent me the MS.—for which I return them my warmest thanks—and I am now to try and give my readers an accurate transcript of its contents.

It is a roll numbered C 246 in the Chapter archives. It is about 9½ inches wide and 8 feet 10 inches long, and consists of three skins now fastened together with pins (which seem to be quite a hundred years old). The writing is very large and clear, and belongs, I think, to the early part of the fourteenth century. Unless I am much mistaken, the hand might very well be the same as that of the great Inventory of Prior Henry of Eastry (Cotton MS. Galba, E. IV.). The titles, and some other parts of the text (but not the verses) are either rubricated, or underlined with red. This I shall express by the use of leaded and italic types. There is no general heading: the writing begins so near the top of the roll that it is quite possible that an original title has been cut off. Indeed, in the transcript referred to there is a title which I expect was originally inscribed at the top of our roll. It is: *Fenestrae in superiori parte ecclesiae Christi Cant. incipientes a parte septentrionali.* The largeness of the writing suggests to me the conjecture that the roll may have been hung up in the Church itself for the perusal of visitors, just as "tables" containing lists of relics, short histories of the foundation, and particulars about distinguished persons buried there, were hung up in various churches. A specimen of such a table, from Glastonbury Abbey, is, I believe, now at Naworth. These documents were generally written upon parchment and affixed to boards.

This roll was not the only form in which the verses were preserved. In the Catalogue of the Library made under Prior Henry of Eastry, printed in Edwards's *Memoirs of Libraries,* vol. I., we have (on p. 167) the entry

Versus pannorum pendencium in ecclesia Cantuariensi
Versus fenestrarum vitrearum ecclesie Christi Cantuar.

and again on p. 216

Versus fenestrarum vitrearum ecclesie Christi.

The verses evidently enjoyed some reputation in their native dlace: and this is the less surprising when we realize that they formed in fact one of the most extensive and complete sets of types and antitypes which were to be found in any English church; and, further, that England was the country in which this special product of medievalism found its most copious expression in artistic monuments. It should also be remembered that the inscriptions on the windows themselves were (and are) exceedingly hard to read.

It has been a matter of some difficulty to decide exactly how the text of the roll ought to be printed. The scribe, though a good writer, was either a careless or a stupid man, and I may remark in passing that this fact tends to confirm my notion that he was the person who wrote Prior Henry of Eastry's inventory, for the catalogue of books which occurs in that teems with foolish mistakes. In copying out the verses on his roll this scribe of ours has done his best to impair its usefulness by misplacing considerable portions of his text. How this can have happened I am unable to see very clearly. It might be conjectured that his archetype consisted of a number of loose slips, or of another roll whose membranes had been fastened together in the wrong order; but in fact neither of these suppositions is confirmed by an examination of the character of the mistakes. The mistakes are there, in any case, and they attracted attention at an early date: a corrector in the fourteenth century has noted some of the most glaring, but I am inclined to suspect that some have eluded him. The misplacements which have been detected are as follows:

In the 3rd window are two small portions of the 6th.

In the 6th window is a large portion of the 8th.

In the 8th window is a large portion of the 9th.

The misplacements which I only suspect concern the 9th, 10th, and 12th windows, and shall not be described yet.

The text before us is also guilty of divers small corruptions which are noticed in footnotes; and I have no doubt that in some cases there are omissions of verses. I have decided that it is on the whole safer to print the text of the roll just as it stands, and to call attention to the detected errors where they occur, by means of brackets and notes. I have added a survey in diagrammatic form of what I suppose each window to have contained. My text is not a line-for-line transcript, but I have indicated how much each line of the roll contains.

As to the date and style of the glass with which we are concerned, the reader should consult the *Notes* I have mentioned and also Mr Westlake's *History of Design in Painted Glass*. All that need be said here is that the glass is of about the middle of the thirteenth century.

THE SUBJECTS OF THE WINDOWS.

Speaking generally, these twelve windows form a well-defined series illustrating the Life of Christ, from the Annunciation to the Resurrection, with a series of types taken from the Old Testament and from other sources. This series bears all the marks of having been thought out at one time, very probably by one man. There is reason to suppose that it, or our record of it, is incomplete. The last window carries the story only so far as the Resurrection of Christ, and intercalates at that point a number of scenes from the Life of St Gregory, instead of giving us—what we have a right to expect—the appearances after the Resurrection, the Ascension, and perhaps the coming of the Holy Ghost and the Last Judgment. We cannot at present tell to what the incompleteness is due.

The series considered as a whole finds its counterpart in many well-known instances. Considered in detail, it differs importantly from any that is known to me. The salient point, to which I find no parallel elsewhere, is the full treatment accorded to the Parables of our Lord. Eight of these are illustrated as copiously as their character admits. There is only one among them which I find handled in the same fashion anywhere else. Here is a rather interesting phenomenon : it shall be examined somewhat more closely.

The parables illustrated in the Canterbury windows are those of (1) the Sower, (2) the Leaven, (3) the Net, (4) the Tares, (5) the Lost Sheep, (6) the Unjust Debtor, (7) the Wedding Garment, (8) the Good Samaritan.

Among the many windows in foreign cathedrals which can be compared in date and character to those we are considering, I find that only three parables are illustrated with any frequency. My survey, I ought to say, includes Chartres, Bourges, Sens, Troyes, Auxerre, Le Mans, as well as a good many churches less rich in thirteenth century glass. I find among these, windows devoted to the Parables of the Good Samaritan, the Prodigal Son, and Dives and Lazarus. One church, that of Bourges, adds two to the list, the Rich Fool, and the Unjust Judge, but it stands alone, so far as I can discover. The first named is the only one that is accompanied with types. Good Samaritan windows are to be seen at Chartres, Bourges, Sens and perhaps elsewhere. The selection of illustrative types in all the examples that I am acquainted with, is very close to that of the Canterbury windows. In this case I have little doubt that the Canterbury designer incorporated an already made pattern into his series. For the other parables, I think he may himself be held responsible.

The subject of the illustration of the Parables in early art would be worth studying specially and separately. My present impression about the matter is that except in the Eastern Church and in such isolated examples as I have mentioned, medieval artists left this rich mine of material practically unworked. One or two subjects must be excepted : the story of Dives and Lazarus occurs frequently in Books of Hours as an illustration to the Office of the Dead. The Return of the Prodigal Son, the Shepherd bringing back the Lost Sheep, the finding of the Lost Piece of Silver, are employed as types in the *Speculum Humanae Salvationis* and the *Biblia Pauperum*. The Ten Virgins are frequently seen on the sculptured portals of the Continent (and at Wells) as pendants to the scene of the Last Judgment. The Good Shepherd—so conspicuous in the earliest Christian art—is an unfamiliar figure in the Middle Ages.

Not until the Renaissance was far advanced do we find painters drawing their themes from the Parables and pictures of the Sower, the Prodigal Son, and the Good Samaritan ; and it seems that a large part of their attractiveness was due to their possibilities as *genre* subjects. For continuous illustration of single parables we have to turn to the works of the sixteenth century engravers.

I remarked in passing that the Eastern Church did not omit the parables from its cycle of sacred subjects: at the same time, it did not treat them from the external point of view. A reference to the manual for the use of painters will show that the meaning of the parable was the chief interest. This was illustrated almost to the exclusion of the story by which the meaning was conveyed. I cannot discern that Byzantine art had in this department any strong influence on the Western designers.

To write the history of the allegorical interpretation of the Old Testament and its application in art to the illustration of the New is not my task in the present tract. It is my function only to shape a stone which may take its place in that larger structure. I may not even spend time in tracing out the first appearance of the various types which come before us in the Canterbury windows. All that I propose to do in these pages is to point out certain recurrences of the same subjects in other similar cycles of pictures. Foremost among these is the great collection of types, made apparently late in the twelfth or early in the thirteenth century and called *Pictor in Carmine*. An edition of this text I have long planned ; and I hope that it may appear at no distant date. All the copies of it which I have so far discovered are of English origin, and I am strongly inclined to believe that the compiler was an Englishman. It seems, indeed, as if at this particular period, the interest in illustrative types was specially active in English monastic circles. The extensive series of paintings which adorned the stalls at Peterborough, the paintings in the chapter-house of Worcester, and the twelve Canterbury windows, are works to which it would be difficult to find parallels in other countries. Each of them is a remarkable series of types and antitypes, and all were produced within a hundred years. It will be worth while to mark the extent to which the Peterborough paintings, the Canterbury windows, and the *Pictor in Carmine* coincide.

We will take the Canterbury windows as our basis:

Window I.

In the first of these, the types of the Annunciation, Visitation, and Nativity are of the commonest kind and are found in all the series I have mentioned.

The *Angel and the Shepherds* has no proper type, but only the figures of two prophets, with inscribed scrolls. These same prophets and legends occur at Peterborough, but not in the *Pictor*, which takes no note of prophets and prophecies.

Window II.

In the second window, Balaam as a type of the Magi belongs to the common stock. Isaiah is at Peterborough and also at Canterbury. The Exodus is in *Pictor* and at Peterborough. Christ and the Gentiles in neither.

Joseph and his brethren		Peterborough	
The Queen of Sheba	Pictor	Peterborough	
Lot	Pictor	Peterborough	
The prophet of 1 K. xiii.	Pictor	Peterborough	
Melchizedek	O		
Samuel	Pictor	Peterborough	Worcester
David flees from Saul	Pictor	Peterborough	
Elijah from Ahab	Pictor	Peterborough	
Massacre of Benjamites	Pictor		
Massacre of Priests at Nob	Pictor		

Window III.

Moses and Jethro		Peterborough
Daniel and Elders	Pictor	Peterborough
The Ark		Peterborough
The Red Sea		Peterborough
Eve tempted (thrice)	Pictor	Peterborough
David and Goliath	Pictor	Peterborough

Window IV.

Adam and Eve cover themselves	Pictor
Israel under the Law	O
The six ages of the world	Pictor

The six ages of man	Pictor
Peter and the Jews	Pictor
Paul and the Gentiles	Pictor
Esdras reads the Law	Pictor
Gregory ordains readers	Pictor (a bishop, not specified)
The Doctors of the Church	O
Moses receives the Law	Pictor
Paul baptizes	O
Naaman cleansed	(Naaman at Elisha's gate. Pictor)

Window V.

Angel binding devil	O
Drusiana's charity	O
Peter fishing, John reading	O
Jacob with Leah and Rachel	Pictor
The Gospel-mill	O
Peter and Paul	O
Jacob at the well	Pictor
Eliezer and Rebecca	Pictor

Window VI.

The only subject found in *Pictor* is the feeding of the five thousand: and there is but a partial resemblance in one of the types selected.

Window VII.

There is here again no coincidence in subject with *Pictor*, which omits the Transfiguration (!).

Window VIII.

None of the subjects are in *Pictor*.

Window IX.

Three subjects, but no types, coincide.

Window X.

The subjects are in *Pictor*, but not the types.

Window XI.

David carrying himself	Pictor	
The Manna	Pictor	
Laban washes the camels' feet	Pictor	
Abraham washes the angels' feet	Pictor	Peterborough
Joseph sold		Peterborough

Joab and Abner (Amasa)	Pictor	Peterborough
Job smitten	Pictor	Peterborough (Job and his friends)
Elisha mocked	Pictor	(type of the mocking). Peterborough

Window XII.

Isaac	Pictor	Peterborough
Widow of Zarephath	Pictor	Peterborough
Brazen serpent	Pictor	Peterborough
Red heifer	Pictor	Peterborough
Death of Abel	Pictor	Peterborough
Blood of the Passover	Pictor	Peterborough
Elisha and Shunammite		Peterborough
Vision of Ezek. ix.	Pictor	(as type of Bearing of the Cross). Peterborough
Samson in Gaza	Pictor	
Jonah in the fish	Pictor	
David and bear	Pictor	Peterborough
Samson and lion	O	
Samson and gates	Pictor	Peterborough
Daniel and dragon	Pictor	
Jonah cast up	Pictor	Peterborough
David escapes	Pictor	Peterborough
Lion and cub	Pictor	
Joseph released [1]	Pictor	

It will be observed that in the windows which illustrate the early life of Christ and the Passion the coincidences between Canterbury, *Pictor in Carmine,* and the Peterborough paintings are very numerous, and that they include the obscurer and rarer types as well as the common ones. But in those which illustrate the Ministry and the Parables, the coincidences are practically negligible. In fact the Peterborough series, like the large majority of medieval monuments, passes straight from the Temptation to the Entry into Jerusalem, while the choice of subjects in *Pictor* seems curiously

[1] A good many of the subjects in Window XII are found in the central eastern window in Becket's crown, nearly the whole of which is old glass. The occurrence of the same subjects more than once in the same church is not by any means uncommon.

capricious and incomplete. As we have seen, the Trans-figuration is omitted.

It is difficult to believe that the Peterborough series is altogether disconnected with that of Canterbury. Not only do the subjects agree to a large extent, but in twenty-one cases—all in the first three windows—the legends are the same. I have at present no copy of the legends of the latter part of the Peterborough series, but I should expect to find coincidences there as well. The Peterborough paintings were of the twelfth century; the Canterbury windows of the thirteenth. Had Benedict, monk of Christ Church and subsequently Abbot of Peterborough, any hand in communicating copies of the Peterborough legends to his old monastery? It seems not unlikely. I am confirmed in my belief in the connexion by the fact that in spite of the coincidences in subject between *Pictor* and the Canterbury series there is hardly any coincidence in the legends, and this though *Pictor* usually gives more verses than two for each subject. For the beginning and end of his series, then, we may allow the probability that the Canterbury designer derived help from Peterborough; but for the middle portion we cannot trace any source.

If we pursue the subject of Typology down to a later date, we find that the tendency to neglect the story of the Ministry in favour of the Infancy and the Passion is on the increase. In the *Biblia Pauperum* the only subjects between the Temptation and the Entry into Jerusalem are the Transfiguration, and the Raising of Lazarus, and Mary Magdalene washing Christ's feet. In the *Speculum Humanae Salvationis* we have only the last-named subject.

In so late a series as the windows of King's College Chapel the Raising of Lazarus is the one subject. The Return of the Prodigal occurs as a type, as also in the *Speculum*.

We have not, as yet, I think, sufficient material before us to pronounce very definitely and dogmatically upon the matter: but at present I hold that in the twelfth and thirteenth centuries a special interest in the collection of types for artistic purposes was a feature of English art in particular, and that the most extensive works in this kind were to be seen in English churches. On the Continent we find such works chiefly confined to smaller areas. Single windows—not a whole series of windows—altar-pieces, such as the retable of Kloster-Neuburg: here and there, as at Laon, a single portal. It was the commonest practice to take an episode of Old Testament history and illustrate that, leaving the connexion between it and the New Testament to be expounded *viva voce*. Such continuous Bible histories are to be seen at Venice, Auxerre, Chartres, Toledo, Rouen, Lyons, Bourges, Orvieto, Pisa, Assisi, in mosaic, sculpture, glass, or fresco, while the collection of types and antitypes on a large scale appears in the thirteenth century in *books* such as the famous *Bible figurée*, of one copy of which portions are to be seen at Paris, London, and Oxford[1]. The *Speculum* and the *Biblia Pauperum* are compilations of the fourteenth century. These are hasty generalizations, but, as I believe, not incorrect ones.

In short, I have searched for evidence of the existence on the Continent in the twelfth and thirteenth centuries of collections of types and antitypes comparable to those of Peterborough, Canterbury, and the *Pictor in Carmine*, and have not found them. For the present, then, I am constrained to say that I regard them as specially characteristic of England.

My last task is to furnish elucidations of those subjects in the Canterbury windows which are likely to be obscure at first sight to the reader. I will put them in the form of notes.

Window IV. 4. *The six ages of the world.* These are represented in this picture by figures of Adam, Noah, Abraham, David, Jechonias, Christ.

Window V. *An angel binds a devil.* I take this to be a representation of Raphael binding Asmodeus in the uttermost parts of Egypt. (Tobit viii. 3.)

Drusiana feeds the poor. Drusiana was a lady of Ephesus converted by John the Evangelist, and subsequently raised by him from the dead. Her story is told in full in the Leucian *Acts of John.*

[1] On this the article by M. Delisle in *Hist. Littéraire*, vol. xxxii, should be consulted.

Peter fishing, John reading. Peter and John are here taken—like Martha and Mary, Leah and Rachel—as types of the active and the contemplative life.

A mill and oven; the Apostles making bread. This subject is comparable with one that appears in later art, of Christ in a wine-press, and the Apostles distributing the wine that flows thence to the world. In later art the picture of the mill is applied specially to the Eucharist. It occurs for instance in a window at Berne, where the Apostles are making Hosts out of the flour. Here at Canterbury, as we see from the inscription, the upper and lower millstones represent the two Testaments and the bread is simply the word of Christ.

Window VI. *The rich of the world.* In the picture, part of which still exists, names are given to the two figures of rich men, namely, Julianus and Mauricius. I have not yet been able to ascertain who are meant.

Window VIII. 15. *Quidam sequuntur regem, quidam fugiunt.* It is not easy to see from the inscription whether the king meant here is the king in the Parable, or whether some subject unconnected with the Parable is intended. If the latter is the case, the particular subject is still obscure.

Window X. 3. Constantine afflicted with leprosy had been recommended to take a bath of children's blood. Silvester dissuaded him from the commission of this cruelty.

6. Theophilus had sold his soul to the devil. The most famous of all the miracles attributed to the Virgin was her recovery of the bond from the devil, and consequent deliverance of Theophilus, who died penitent within a few days.

The three dead persons raised in this window typify three degrees of sin. Jairus' daughter dead in the house, is the evil thought. The widow's son, outside the city gate, is the evil act. Lazarus, already in the tomb, is the confirmed habit of sin. The two verses which set this forth are very commonly found scribbled on fly-leaves in medieval manuscripts.

Window XI. David bearing himself in his hands. This curious type is founded ultimately on the LXX. version of the title of Ps. xxxiv., where the words, translated in the A. V. by "changed his behaviour," are rendered παρεφέρετο ἐν ταῖς χερσὶν αὐτοῦ. This the Latin translates "ferebatur in manibus suis," and Augustine (commenting on the Psalm in question), perhaps for the first time applies this to the illustration of the Last Supper, where Christ carried Himself in His own hands. A medieval critic annotating the *Pictor in Carmine* understands it of David dancing before the Ark, suggesting that he may have stood on his head on that occasion, and so practically have borne himself in his hands.

(*P*)*rima fenestra.*

Moises cum rubo.   In medio angelus cum maria[1]. |
  Rubus non consumitur
  tua nec comburitur
    in carne uirginitas. |
Gedeon cum uellere et conca.
  Vellus celesti rore maduit.
  dum puelle | uenter intumuit.
Misericordia et ueritas.   In medio maria et elizabet. |
  Plaude puer puero uirgo uetule quia uero |
  Obuiat hic pietas.   ueteri dat lex noua metas.   *Justicia et pax.* |
  Applaudit regi preuisor gr*ati*a legi. |
  Oscula iusticie dat pax cognata marie[2].
Nabugodonosor et lapis cum | statua.   Puer in presepio.
  Vt regi uisus lapis e*st* de monte recisus. |
  In medio maria.   Sic grauis absque uiro uirgo parit ordine
    miro[3]. |
Moyses cum uirga.   In medio angelus et pastores. |
  Vt contra morem dedit arida uirgula florem. |
  Sic uirgo puerum uerso parit ordine rerum[4].
Dauid.   Gaudebunt | campi et omnia que in eis sunt.
Abacuc.   Operuit celos gloria eius, etc. |

(*F*)*enestra secunda.*

In medio tres reges equitantes.
Balaam.   Orietur | stella ex Jacob · et exurget homo de israel.
Ysaias et ierusalem.   Ambulabunt | gentes in lumine tuo, etc.
In medio herodes et magi.
Christus et gentes. | Qui sequuntur me non ambulant in tenebris |
  Stella magos duxit et eos ab herode reduxit. |
  Sic sathanam gentes fugiunt te Christe sequentes[5]. |
Pharao et moyses cum populo exiens ab egypto. |
  Exit ab erumpna populus ducente columpna. |
  Stella magos duxit · lux Christus utrisque reluxit[6].

---

[1] This line is wholly in red.

[2] These four verses occurred on the painted stall-backs at Peterborough. They are recorded in MS. Arundel 30 at the College of Arms.   Instead of *preuisor* in the 3rd line this MS. reads rightly *precursor*.

[3] Also occurred at Peterborough.

[4] Also occurred at Peterborough: for *dedit arida uirgula* the Arundel MS. has *dat amigdalus arida.*

[5] Also at Peterborough.   The variants are *magis luxit*, and *At Sathanam.*

[6] Also at Peterborough.

In medio maria cum | puero. Magi et pastores. Joseph et fratres sui cum egyptiis. |

Ad te longinquos ioseph trahis atque propinquos.
Sic deus in cunis iudeos gentibus unis[1].

Rex salomon et regina saba. |

Hijs donat donis regina domum salomonis. |
Sic reges domino dant munera tres tria trino[1].

Admoniti sunt magi | ne herodem adheant (sic). *propheta et rex.
Jeroboam immolans. |*

Vt uia[2] mutetur redeundo propheta monetur |
Sic tres egerunt qui Christo dona tulerunt[1].

Subuersio sodome et loth fugiens. |

Vt loth saluetur ne respiciat prohibetur. |
Sic uitant reuehi per herodis regna sabei[1].

Oblatio pueri in templo et | symeon.

Melchisedech offerens panem et uinum pro abraham. |

Sacrum quod cernis sacris fuit umbra modernis. |
Vmbra fugit, quare. quia Christus sistitur are[1].

Oblatio samuelis. |

Natura geminum triplex oblatio trinum |
Significat dominum samuel puer amphora uinum[1] [3]

Fuga domini in egip|tum.

Fuga dauid . et doech. |

Hunc saul infestat saul herodis typus exstat. |
Iste typus Christi cuius fuga consonat isti[1].

Helyas. Jezabel et Achab. |

Vt trucis insidias jezabel declinat helyas. |
Sic deus herodem terrore remotus eodem[2].

Occisio innocentium.

Occisio | sacerdotum domini sub saule |

Non cecidit dauid pro quo saul hos iugulauit |
Sic non est cesus cum cesis transfuga ihesus[1].

Occisio tribus beniamin in gabaon. |

Ecce rachel nati fratrum gladiis iugulati |
Hiis sunt signati pueri sub herode necati[1]. |

(F)enestra tercia.

Ihesus sedet in medio doctorum.
Moyses et Jetro cum populo. |

[1] Also at Peterborough.
[2] *uita* corr. to *uia*.
[3] At Peterborough the lines were transposed.

Sic moyses audit jetro uir sanctus obaudit |
Gentiles[1] uerbis humiles sunt forma superbis[2].
Daniel in medio seniorum. |
Mirantur pueri seniores uoce doceri. |
Sic responsa dei sensum <que> stupent pharisei[3].
Baptizatur dominus.
Noe in archa. |
Fluxu cuncta uago submergens prima uorago. |
Omnia purgauit. baptisma[4] significauit[5]
Submersio pharaonis et transitus populi. |
Vnda maris rubri spacio diuisa salubri. |
Que mentem mundam facit a uitio notat undam[6].
Temptatio gule | et uane glorie.
Eua capiens fructum. |
Qui temptat ihesum monet[6] euam mortis ad esum. |
Eua gule cedit sed non ita ihesus obedit[5].
Eua comedit. |
Victor es hic sathana mouet euam gloria uana. |
Sed quo uicisti[7] te uicit gr*ati*a christi. |
Vt goliam dauid sathanam christus superauit[8].
[*De . v . panibus et · ij · piscibus | saciauit multa milia hominum.*
Dominus sacerdos et Rex. |
Hii panes legem pisces dantem sacra regem. |
Signant quassatos a plebe nec adnichilatos[9].]
Temptatio cupiditatis.
Adam et eua comedunt. |
Quo sathan hos subicit sathanam sapiencia uicit. |
[9]*[Synagoga cum moyse et libris.*

[1] *l.* Gentilis.

[2] Also at Peterborough. The first line ran thus:

Hinc homines audit deus . hinc uir sanctus obaudit

In the 2nd line *sint* was read for *sunt.* In the glass itself at Canterbury we find curiously enough the Peterborough reading of l. 1. The names of Moses and Jethro have crept in wrongly, they are inscribed over the heads of the personages.

[3] Also at Peterborough, where *sensumque* was the reading: as it also is in the glass at Canterbury.

[4] Add *que*, as at Peterborough, where the heading was *Mundum purgauit baptisma que sanctificauit* (!): and as the glass at Canterbury.

[5] Also at Peterborough.

[6] *l.* mouet.

[7] Obscurely written: a later hand adds *vicisti* at end of line.

[8] This line is underlined in red, and a slightly later note is attached: *quere in vj[ta] fenestra.*

[9] See Window VI.

Ecclesia cum Johanne.

Non[1] populos saturant panes piscesque figurant. |
Quod testamenta duo nobis dant[2] alimenta.]

(*F*)*enestra iiij*^{a}.

Vocatio natanael iacentis sub ficu.
Adam et eua cum folijs. |
Populus sub lege.

Vidit in hijs christus sub ficu natanaelem. |
Lex tegit hanc plebem quasi ficus natanaelem.

Christus mutauit aquam in | uinum. et sex ydrie.
Sex etates mundi.

Ydria metretas capiens est quelibet etas.
Primum signorum deus hic prodendo suorum.   *Sex etates*
    hominis. |

  · Limpha dat hystoriam uinum notat allegoriam. |
· · In uinum morum conuertit aquam uitiorum.

Piscatores apostolorum[3].
Sanctus petrus cum ecclesia | de iudeis.

Verbum rete ratis petri domus hec pietatis. |
Pisces iudei qui rete ferant pharisei. |

Paulus cum ecclesia de gentibus.

Illa secunda ratis domus hec est plena beatis. |
Recia scismaticus et quiuis scindit iniquus[4].

In medio ihesus legit in syna\goga.
Esdras legit legem populo. |

Quid promulgauit moyses legem reparauit. |
·:· Esdras amissam christus renouauit omissam.

Sanctus gregorius ordinans lectores. |

Quod christus legit quasi pro lectoribus egit. |
Exemplo cuius sacer est gradus ordinis huius.

Sermo domini in monte.

---

[1] ? *l.* qui.
[2] Corrected from *dantur.*
[3] On the glass itself the title is: Piscatio Apostolorum. Rete rumpitur.
[4] The lines read best in this order:

    Verbum rete etc.
    Illa secunda etc.
    Pisces iudei etc.
    Recia etc.

But the error, if error it be, is perpetuated in the glass itself, where the first
two lines exist.

Doctores ecclesie. |
Moyses suscepit legem[1].
>Hij montem scandunt scripture dum sacra pandunt. |
>Christus sublimis docet hos sed vulgus in ymis. |
>Ex (*l.* lex) hinc inde datur in monte quod inde notatur. |
>Christum nouisse debemus utramque dedisse. |

Christus descendens de monte mundat leprosum.
Paulus baptizat populum. |
>Carne deus tectus quasi uallis ad ima prouectus. |
> .:. Mundat leprosum genus humanum uiciosum.

Helyseus Naaman et Ior|danis. |
>Quem lauat ecce deus quem mundat et hic helyseus : |
>Est genus humanum Christi baptismate sanum. |

(*F*)enestra *v*[a].

Ihesus eicit demonium.
Angelus ligauit demonium. |
>Imperat inmundis deus hic <ut> equis furibundis. |
>Hijs uirtus Christi dominatur ut angelus isti.

Maria unxit pedes Christi.
Drusiana | uestit et pascit egenos. |
>Curam languenti uictum qui prebet egenti. |
>Seque reum plangit Christi uestigia tangit. |
>Illa quod unguendo facit hec sua distribuendo. |
>Dum quod de pleno superest largitur egeno. |

Martha et maria cum ihesu.
Petrus in naui.
Iohannes legit. |
>Equoris unda ferit hunc. ille silencia querit. |
>Sic requies orat dum mundi cura laborat.

Lya et Rachel cum iacob. |
>Lya gerit curam carnis Rachelque figuram. |
>Mentis cura grauis est hec est altera suauis. |

Ihesus et apostoli colligunt spicas.
Mola . fumus[2]. *et apostoli facientes panes.* |
>Quod terit alterna mola lex uetus atque moderna |
> .:. Passio crux Christe tua sermo tuus cibus iste.

Petrus et paulus cum populis. |
>Arguit iste reos humiles alit hic phariseos. |
>Sic apice trite panis sunt uerbaque uite.

Ihesus cum Samaritana.
Sy|nagoga et Moyses cum .v. libris. |

---

[1] The rubric applies to the line beginning: *Ex* (*lex*) *hinc.*
[2] *l.* furnus.

Potum quesisti fidei cum christe sitisti |
Equa uiri cui sex synagoga librique sui sex.

Ecclesia[1] *de gentibus ad ihesum.* |

.:. Deli^cta[2] (*sic*) delicta notat ydria fonte relicta. |
Ad te de gente deus ecclesia ueniente.

Samaritana adduxit po pulum ad ihesum.

Rebecca dat potum iacob. |

Fons seruus minans pecus ydria uirgo propinans. |
Lex Christo gentes mulierque fide redolentes.

Jacob obuiat Racheli cum grege.

Jacob lassatus Rachel obuia grex adaquatus. |
Sunt deus et turbe mulier quas duxit ab urbe. |

(*F*)*enestra vj*^*ta*.

Ihesus loquens cum apostolis.

Gentes audiunt.

pharisei contempnunt[3] |

Sollicite gentes stant uerba dei scicientes. |
Hij sunt uerba dei . que contempnunt pharisei. |

Seminator et uolucres

pharisei recedentes a ihesu.

Semen rore carens expers rationis et arens. |
Hij sunt qui credunt temptantos[4] sicque recedunt.

Pharisei temptantes ihesum. |

Semen sermo dei uia lex secus hanc pharisei |
Et tu Christe sator uerbrum (*sic*) patris insidiator[5].

Semen cecidit inter spi|nas.

Diuites huius mundi cum pecunia.

Semen cecidit in terram | bonam.

Isti spinosi locupletes deliciosi. |
Nil fructus referunt quoniam terrestria querunt.

Ioh. Daniel. Noe. ce. in ter. bo.[6] |

Verba patris seuit deus hijs fructus sibi creuit. |
In tellure bona triplex sua cuique corona.

Ihesus et mulier commiscens | sata tria.

tres filii noe cuu ecclesia.

Virgines . continentes . coniugati . |

---

[1] Ec͞c͞ca.

[2] *l.* Deleta, in spite of the false quantity involved.

[3] *contempnunt* added by a later hand.

[4] *l.* temptantur.

[5] ? uerbi patris insinuator.

[6] i.e. ceciderunt (*or* cemen *for* semen) in terram bonam.

Parte noe nati michi quisque sua dominati. |
Vna fides natis ex hiis tribus est deitatis. |
Persone trine tria sunt sata muta[1] farine. |
Fermentata sata tria tres fructus operata. |
Piscatores. hinc pisces boni inde mali. |
Hij qui iactantur in leuam qui reprobantur. |
Pars est a domino maledicta cremanda camino.
Isti in uitam eternam. |
Vase reseruantur pisces quibus assimulantur. |
Hij quos addixit uite deus et benedixit.
*Messores . seges . Reponitur | in horreum . Zizania in ignem.
justi in uitam eternam.*
*Reprobi in ignem e*ternum. |
Cum sudore sata messoris in horrea lata. |
Sunt hic uexati sed Christo glorificati. |
Hic cremat ex messe quod inutile iudicat esse. |
Sic prauos digne punit iudex deus igne.
⌈*Rex fecit nupcias filio et misit seruos*[2]. |
Rex pater ad natum regem sponse sociatum. |
Precipit asciri populos renuuntque uenire. |
Excusant se quidam per villam.
Quos uexat cura caro · quinque boum iuga rura. |
Nuncius excusans . hic ortans ille recusans. |
Petrus docens sed sequuntur moysen et synagogam.
Sunt ascire uolens deus hunc hic credere nolens. |
Petrus[3] docens isti[4]que studens iudea fuisti[5]. |
Johannes preiudicat[6] intente audientibus.
Vox inuitantis cause tres dissimulantis. |
Sponsam sponsus amat : uox horam preuia clamat. |
Ysaias predicat audientibus turbis.
Ecclesiam Christe iunctam tibi predicat iste. |
Hiis imitata gens est ad edenda parata. |
Quidam sequuntur regem quidam fugiunt.
Hic . Regis[7] . factum confirmat apostolus actum. |
Credit et accedit cito gens iudea recedit.
Contemplatur rex come|dentes.

[1] *l.* mista, as edd.
[2] Above this, in a slightly later hand, is the note: *non hic sed in octaua fenestra.*
[3] *l.* Petre.
[4] *isti* corr. from *istis.*
[5] *fuisti* from *fuistis.*
[6] sc. *predicat.*
[7] Regis added over erasure by a hand of cent. xv early (?).

Resurgunt mortui. |
Ad mensam tandem cito plebs sedet omnis eandem |
Sic om*n*es eadem uox hora cogit eadem.
Dominus dicit electis · Venite benedicti. |
Rex plebem pauit spretis quos ante uocauit. |
Christus se dignos reficit · reicitque malignos.
Inuenitur et eicitur non vestitus ueste nupciali. |
Diues et extrusus seruus tenebrisque reclusus. |
Quem condempnauit rex eiecit cruciauit.
Ananias et saphira mo|riuntur a petro.
∟*Dominus eiecit uendentes a templo.* |

(*F*)*enestra vij*^a^.

Curauit ihesus filiam uidue.
Ecclesia de gentibus cum ihesu. |
Natam cum curat matris prece matre figurat |
Christo credentes primos · nataque sequentes.
Petrus orat et animalia | dimittuntur in linthea[1]. |
Fide uiuentes signant animalia gentes. |
Quos mundat sacri submersio trina lauacri.
Curauit ihesus hominem ad | piscinam.
moyses cum quinque libris. |
Lex tibi piscina concordat[2] quia quina |
Hostia piscine seu partes lex tibi quine.
Baptizat dominus. |
Sanat ut egrotum piscine motio lotum.
Sic cruce signatos mundat baptisma renatos. |
Transfiguratio domini
angeli uestiunt mortuos resurgentes. |
Spes transformati capitis spes uiuificati. |
Claret in indutis membris a morte solutis.
Adducunt angeli iustos ad deum. |
Cum transformares te Christe quid insinuares |
Veste decorati declarant clarificati.
Petrus piscatur et inuenit staterem |
Dominus ascendit in ierusalem.
Hunc ascend<ente>m mox mortis adesse uidentem. |
Tempora te Christe piscis prenunciat iste.

---

[1] *a* erased.
[2] Insert cur ? and read:

> Lex tibi piscina concordat. Cur ? quia quina
> Ostia etc.

Dominus crucifigitur in cruce factus. |
    Ludibrium turbe deus est eiectus ab urbe[1].
Statuit ihesus paruulum in | *medio discipulorum.*
Monachi lauant pedes pauperum. |
    Hoc informantur exemplo qui monachantur. |
    Ne dedignentur peregrinis si famulentur.
Reges inclinantur doctrine Petri et Pauli. |
    Sic incuruati puero sunt assimulati. |
    Reges cum gente . paulo petroque docente.
Pastor sine uersu repor|tat ouem.
Christus pendet in cruce.
Christus spoliat infernum. |

(*F*)enestra viij[a].

Dominus remittit debita seruo poscenti. |
    Vt prece submissa sunt hinc[2] commissa remissa. |
    Parcet poscenti seu parcit deus egenti.
Petrus et paulus absoluunt | *penitentem et dominus sibi credentes.*
Seruus percutit conseruum.
Paulus lapidatur. |
    Cui plus ignoscit dominus minus ille poposcit. |
    Conseruus[3] seruus populus te paule proteruus.
Stephanus lapidatur. |
    Regi conseruo repetenti debita seruo. |
    Assimulare deus martyr nequam phariseus.
Tradidit eum tortoribus. |
    Ceditur affligens captiuatur crucifigens. |
    Hunc punit dominus flagris hos igne caminus. |
Mittuntur impii in ignem.
Judei perimuntur.
⌐*Mittit dominus duos disci|pulos propter asinam et pullum[4].* |
    Imperat adduci pullum cum matre magister. |
    Paruit hunc[5] opera succinctus uterque minister. |
Spiritus sanctus in specie columbe inter deum et hominem. |
    Signacius[6] simplex quod sit dilectio duplex. |
    Ala deum dextra fratrem docet ala sinistra.
Ihesus stans inter Petrum et paulum. |
    Genti que seruit petris petrum petra mittit |
    Escas diuinas iudeis paule propinas.

---

[1] Rubric and legend both seem defective.
[2] *l.* huic.   [3] *l.* conseruum.
[4] Note above this in slightly later hand: *non hic sed in nona fenestra.*
[5] *l.* huic.   [6] *l.* Signat auis.

Adducunt discipuli asinam et pullum. |
    Que duo soluuntur duo sunt animalia bruta. |
    Ducitur ad christum pullus materque soluta.
Petrus adducit ecclesiam de gentibus. |
    De populo fusco petri sermone corusco |
    Extrahit ecclesiam ueram reserando sophiam. |
Paulus ducit ecclesiam de gentibus[1].
    Sic radio fidei ceci radiantur hebrei. |
    Per pauli uerba fructum sterilis dedit herba. |
    Dum plebs gentilis per eum fit mente fidelis. |
    Gentilis populus uenit ad Christum quasi pullus.
Occur<r>unt pueri domino sedenti super asinam. |
    Vestibus ornari patitur saluator asellam. |
    Qui super astra sedet. nec habet frenum neque sellam. |
Ysaias dicit. Ecce rex tuus sedens super asinam. |
    Qui sedet in celo ferri dignatur asello.
Dauid . Ex ore infantium etc. |
L   Sancti sanctorum laus ore sonat puerorum. |

(F)enestra ix[a].

Homo quidam descendebat de ierusalem in Jerico et incidit in latrones. |
    Perforat hasta latus occidit ad mala natus.
Creatur adam.
forma‚tur eua
comedunt fructum
eiciuntur de paradiso. |
    Ex ade costa prodijt formata uirago. |
    Ex Christi latere processit sancta propago. |
    Fructum deserpens[2] mulier suadens mala serpens. |
    Inmemor auctoris uir perdunt culmen honoris. |
    Virgultum . fructus . mulier . uir . uipera . luctus . |
    Plantatur . rapitur . dat . gustat . fallit . initur . |
    Pena reos tangit uir sudat femina plangit, |
    Pectore portatur serpens tellure cibatur.
Sacerdos et leuita uident | *wlneratum et pertranseunt.* |
    Vulneribus plenum neuter miseratus[3] egenum. |
    Cui color est rubeus si[4] cum mare transit hebreus |
    Angelico ductu patet in medio uia fluctu. |
    In ligno serpens positum notat in cruce Christum. |
    Qui uidet hunc uiuit . uiuet qui credit in istum. |

[1] sic: *l.* iudeis.
[2] corr. later to decerpens. *c* written above *s*.
[3] *l.* miseratur.   [4] *l.* sic.

Cernens quod. speciem deitatis dum teret aurum
Frangit scripta tenens moyses in puluere taurum.
Moyses et aaron | cum pharaone.
scribitur tau.
educitur populus.
adorat uitulum. |
datur lex.
eleuatur serpens. |

Pro populo moyses coram pharaone laborat. |
Exaugeatque preces signorum luce coronat.
Samaritanus ducit | vulneratum in stabulum cum jumento.
prohicio[1] ihesu.
ancilla accu|sat petrum.
dominus crucifigitur.
sepelitur.
resurgit.
loquitur angelus ad marias. |

Qui caput est nostrum capitur qui regibus ostrum |
Predet[2] nudatur qui soluit uincla ligatur. |
In ligno pendens . in ligno brachia tendens. |
In ligno lignum superasti Christe malignum. |
Christum lege rei liuor condempnat hebrei. |
Carne flagellatum rapit attrahit ante pilatum. |
Solem iusticie tres orto sole marie |
Querunt lugentes ex eius morte trementes. |

(*F*)*enestra* x^a.

Suscitat ihesus puellam in domo. |
Que iacet in cella surgens de morte puella. |
Signat peccatum meditantis corde creatum.
Abigail occurrit dauid et mutat eius propositum. |
Rex dauid arma gerit dum nabal perdere querit. |
Obuiat abigail mulcet dauid arma refrenat. |
Et nebulam vultus hilari sermone serenat. |
Constantinus iacens et matres cum pueris. |
Rex soboles helene . Romane rector habene.
Vult mundare cutem querendo cruce[3] salutem. |
Nec scelus excercet . flet . humet[4] dictata cohercet.
Dominus suscitat puerum extra portam. |
Qui iacet in morte puer extra limina porte. |
Deforis abstractum peccati denotat actum.

[1] sc. proditio.
[3] *l.* cruore.

[2] *l.* Prebet.
[4] *l.* fletum et.

Rex salomon adorat y|dola et *deflet peccatum.*
Errat femineo salomon deceptus amore. |
Errorem redimit mens saucto tacta dolore.
Penitencia theophili. |
 Dum lacrimando gemit theophilus acta redemit. |
 Inuenies[1] ueniam dulcem rogando[2] mariam.
Dominus suscitat Lazarum. |
 Mens mala mors intus malus actus : mors foris : vsus. |
 Tumba puella puer lazarus ista notant.
Angelus alloquitur ionam sub edera ante niniuem. |
 Pingitur hic niniue iam pene peracta[3] perire. |
Penitentia marie egipciace |
 Veste fide zozimas nudam tegit[4] mariam. |

(*F*)*enestra xj.*

In medio cena domini.
Dauid gestans se in manibus suis. |
 Quid manibus dauid se gestans significauit. |
 Te manibus gestans das Christe tuis manifestans.
Manna fluit populo de celo. |
 Manna fluit saturans populum de plebe figurans |
 De mensa ihesum dare se cenantibus esum.
Lauat ihesus pedes apostolorum.
Laban lauat pedes camelorum.
 Cum laban hos curat typice te Christe figurat |
 Cura camelorum mandatum discipulorum.
Abraham lauat pedes angelorum. |
 Obsequio lauacri notat hospes in hospite sacri. |
 Quos mundas sacro mundasti Christe lauacro.
Proditio ihesu.
Vendicio joseph. |
 Fraus Jude Christum fraus fratrum uendidit istum. |
 Hij iude Christi Joseph tu forma fuisti.
Joab osculatur Abner et occidit. |
 Federa dum fingit ioab in funera stringit. |
 Ferrum iudaicum presignans fedus iniquum.
Vapulatio ihesu.
Job percussus ulcere. |
 Christi testatur plagas Job dum cruciatur. |
 Vt sum[5] iudee iocus[6] pueris helisee. |

---

[1] Inueniens.   [2] rogitando.
[3] parata.   [4] *add* ecce.
[5] ? tu.   [6] *add* es.

(*F*)enestra xij$^\alpha$.

Christus portat crucem.
Ysaac ligna.
mulier colligit duo ligna
Christus suspenditur. |

    Ligna puer gestat crucis[1] typum manifestat. |
    Fert crucis in signum duplex muliercula lignum.
Serpens eneus eleuatur in columpna. |

    Mors est exanguis dum cernitur eneus anguis. |
    Sic deus in ligno nos saluat ab hoste maligno.
Vacca rufa comburitur. |

    Vt moyses iussit uitulam rufam rogus ussit. |
    Sic tua Christe caro crucis igne crematur amaro.
Dominus deponitur de ligno. |
Abel occiditur.
Heliseus expandit se super puerum.

    Nos a morte deus reuocauit et hunc heliseus. |
    Signat abel christi pia funera funere tristi.
Moyses scribit tau . in frontibus in porta de sanguine agni.

    Rex moritur magnus forma cuius extitit agnus. |
    [2]Frontibus infixum thau . precinuit crucifixum.
Dominus in sepulcro.
Samson dormit cum amica sua. |

    Vt sampson typice causa dormiuit amice. |
    Ecclesie causa Christi caro marmore clausa.
Jonas in uentre ceti. |

    Dum iacet absortus jonas sol triplicat ortus. |
    Sic deus artatur tumulo triduoque moratur.
Dominus ligans diabolum spoli|auit infernum.
Dauid eripuit oues.
et Sampsonson[3] tulit portas. |

    Saluat ouem dauid sic Christum significauit. |
    Est sampson fortis qui rupit vincula mortis.
Sampson frangit ora leonis
et daniel draconis.

    Instar sampsonis frangit deus ora leonis. |
    Dum sathanam strauit Christus regulum iugulauit.

---

[1] *add* unde. The line, thus emended, occurred in the Chapter-house at Worcester.

[2] This verse occurred in the Chapter-house at Worcester.

[3] *sic.*

Surgit dominus de sepulcro. |
Jonas eicitur de pisce[1].

    [2]Redditur ut saluus quem ceti clauserat aluus. |
    Sic redit illesus *a mortis carcere*[3] ihesus.

Dauid emissus per fenestram. |

    Hinc abit illesus dauid sic *inuida*[4] ihesus |
    Agmina conturbat vt uicta morte resurgat.

Angelus alloquitur mariam | *ad sepulcrum.*

leo suscitat filium
et Joseph extrahitur[5] *de carcere.* |

    Ad uitam Christum deus ut leo suscitat istum.
    Te signat Christe ioseph . te mors . locus iste. |

(S)anctus Gregorius dat aquam manibus pauperum et apparuit ei
      dominus. |

    Hospes abest vbi sit stupet hic cur quoue resistit. |
    Membra prius quasi me suscepistis sed heri me. |

Gregorius dictat . Petrus scribit.
Solitarius cum cato. |

    Pluris habes catum quam presul pontificatum. |
    Que liber includit signata columba recludit. |

Hostia mutatur in formam digiti. |

    Id panis velat digiti quod forma reuelat. |
    Velans forma redit cum plebs abscondita credit. |

Gregorius trahitur et papa[6] *efficitur.* |

    Quem nomen . vultus . lux . vita . sciencia . cultus. |
    Approbat extractus latebris fit *papa*[6] coactus. |

Explicit. |

THE ARRANGEMENT OF THE WINDOWS.

We will now set forth in tabular form the contents of each
of these twelve windows, taking into account the corrections in
the roll, and also the extant remains of the glass in so far as
these last enable us by their form to shew the arrangement
of the subjects.

---

[1] These two lines were probably meant to be transposed.
[2] This line occurred in the Chapter-house at Worcester.
[3] Corr. from *dauid sic inuida.*
[4] Corr. from *iuda.*   [5] *l.* extrahitur.
[6] *papa* is blotted out.

Window I.

1 Moses and the Burning Bush.
2 The Annunciation.
3 Gideon and the Fleece.
4 Mercy and Truth meet (Ps. lxxxv. 10).
5 The Visitation.
6 Righteousness and Peace kiss each other.
7 The Stone cut out without hands (Dan. ii. 34).
8 The Nativity.
9 Aaron's rod, held by Moses.
10 David with scroll (Ps. xcv. (xcvi.) 12).
11 The angel and the shepherds.
12 Habakkuk with scroll (Hab. iii. 3).

Window II [1].

1 *Balaam.
2 *The Three Kings on their way to Judaea.
3 *Isaiah and Jerusalem (Is. lx.).
4 *The Exodus: the Pillar of Fire.
5 *Herod and the Three Kings.
6 *Christ leading the Gentiles.
7 *The Queen of Sheba visits Solomon.
8 *The Three Kings adore Christ.
9 *Joseph reverenced by his brethren and by the Egyptians.
10 *Sodom overthrown: Lot warned not to look back.
11 *The Three Kings warned to go back another way.
12 *The Prophet of 1 K. xiii., and Jeroboam sacrificing. "Nor turn again by the same way that thou camest."
13 *Samuel presented at Shiloh.
14 *The Presentation of Christ in the Temple.
15 Melchizedek and Abraham.
16 David flees from Saul: Doeg sees him.
17 The Flight into Egypt.
18 Elijah flees from Jezebel and Ahab.
19 Saul kills the priests at Nob.
20 Massacre of the Innocents.
21 The Benjamites slain (Judg. xx.).

[1] The subjects marked with an asterisk still exist.

Window III[1].

1 *Moses hearkens to Jethro's advice.

2 *Jesus and the Doctors.

3 *Daniel as a youth judges the elders (Hist. Susan.).

4 *Noah in the Ark.

5 Baptism of Christ.

6 [2]The crossing of the Red Sea.

7 Eve plucks the forbidden fruit.

8 The first and second Temptation of Christ (stone, and Temple).

9 Eve eats the fruit.

10 Adam and Eve eat the fruit.

11 The third Temptation (the High Mountain).

12 David conquers Goliath.

Window IV[1].

1 Adam and Eve with fig-leaves.

2 *Nathanael called from under the fig tree.

3 Israel overshadowed by the Law.

4 *The six ages of the world.

5 *The feast of Cana: the six water-pots.

6 *The six ages of man.

7 Paul and the Gentile Church.

8 *The Apostles fishing.

9 *Peter and the Jewish Church.

10 Ezra reads the Law to the people.

11 Jesus reads in the Synagogue at Capernaum.

12 St Gregory ordains readers.

13 Moses receives the Law.

14 The Sermon on the Mount.

15 The Doctors of the Church.

16 Naaman cleansed in Jordan.

17 Jesus, coming down from the Mount, heals a leper.

18 Paul baptizes converts.

The six ages of man are Infantia, Pueritia, Adolescentia, Juventus, Virilitas, Senectus.

The six ages of the world are represented by figures of Adam, Noe, Abrah(am), David, Jechonias, (Jesus).

[1] The subjects marked with an asterisk still exist.
[2] The inscription remains, but not the picture.

Window V.

1 An Angel (? Raphael) binds a devil.	2a Jesus casts out a devil (? out of Mary Magdalene).	2b Mary anoints Jesus' feet.	3 Drusiana (convert of St John) clothes and feeds the poor.
4 Peter fishing, John reading.	5 Jesus at Bethany, with Mary and Martha.		6 Jacob with Leah and Rachel.
7 A mill and an oven: the apostles make bread.	8 Jesus and the apostles gather ears of corn.		9 Peter and Paul preach to Jews and Gentiles.
10 Jacob meets Rachel at the well.	11 Jesus and the woman of Samaria.		12 Rebekah gives drink to Eliezer (*Jacob* in the MS.).
13 Moses with the Law, and the synagogue.	14 The Samaritans brought to Jesus by the woman.		15 The Gentile Church comes to Christ.

In the MS. nos. 10 and 12 occupy the places of nos. 13 and 15. I have interchanged them. Very probably 11 and 14 occupied one medallion.

Mr Austin's restoration of the window is as follows:

Christ casts devils out of two men.	Mary Magdalene washes Christ's feet.	Angel and devil.
Mary Magdalene's charity.		Drusiana's charity.
The woman of Samaria and the Villagers.	Mary, Martha, and Christ.	Peter and John.
The apostles at the mill.		Peter preaching.
Leah, Jacob, and Rachel.	Christ and the woman of Samaria.	Gentile Church and Christ.
Rebekah and Eliezer.		Jacob and Rachel at the well.

This restoration seems to me clearly erroneous in that it omits the subject of Jesus and the Apostles gathering corn and inserts that of Mary Magdalene's charity, which does not appear in the MS. It also upsets the arrangement of type and antitype in the lower part of the window.

Window VI[1].

1 *The Gentiles hearken.	2 Jesus speaks with the apostles.	3 *The Pharisees turn away.
4 Pharisees tempting Jesus.	5 *The Sower: *a*. The birds. | *b*. The seed in shallow ground.	6 *Pharisees departing.
7 *The rich of this world.	8 *The Sower: *a*. The seed among thorns. *b*. The seed in good ground.	9 *Noah, Daniel and Job.
10 *The three sons of Noah.	11 The Three Measures of Meal.	12 *The three estates of Virginity, Continence and Widowhood.
13 The just enter Paradise.	14 The Net: good and bad fish. | The Harvest: wheat and tares.	15 The wicked go to Hell.
16 Jesus as Priest and King.	17 The feeding of the Five Thousand.	18 The Synagogue with Moses, the Church with John.

[1] The subjects marked with an asterisk still exist.

In Mr Austin's restoration the series of subjects is made
to read from below upwards. Thus:

Moses.	Feeding of 5000.	John Baptist.
Wheat in garner.	Reapers.	Hell.
Separating Fish.	Net.	Angels and devils with souls.
Three Estates.	Three Measures of Meal.	Three sons of Noah.
Noah, David, Job.	Sower.	Rich.
Christ preaches.	Sower and birds.	Christ. Jews turn away.
Gentiles.	Christ and apostles.	Pharisees.

This is the window in which the scribe of the roll has
made his worst mistakes. He has inserted nos. 16—18 in
window IV. and has also put a large section of window VIII.
into window VI. Mr Austin is demonstrably wrong in his
placing of nos. 1 and 3, for both pictures still exist and their form
shows that 1 must have been on the left and 3 on the right.

Window VII.

1 The Gentile Church with Jesus.

2 Jesus heals the Syrophoenician's daughter.

3 The Vision of Peter (Acts x.).

4 Moses with the books of the Law.

5 The man healed at Bethesda.

6 Christ baptizing.

7 Angels clothe the rising dead.

8 The Transfiguration.

9 Angels bring souls to God.

10 Peter finds the stater in the fish's mouth.

11 Jesus goes up to Jerusalem.

12 ? The Crucifixion.

13 Monks wash the feet of the poor.

14 A child set in the midst of the apostles.

15 Kings obey the teaching of Peter and Paul.

16 Christ on the Cross.

17 The Shepherd brings back the Lost Sheep.

18 The Harrowing of Hell.

Nos. 10—12 cause a difficulty. It is not clear from the roll whether 10 or 11 ought to be the central subject: but as the fish is said in the verse to be the type of Christ, I have placed it on the left. Both the title and the legend of no. 12 seem incomplete. The title is *Dominus crucifigitur in cruce factus:* and the legend has only one line instead of two. " God, made a mocking-stock of the multitude, is cast out of the city."

No. 17 is said in the roll to have had no legend: and the statement seems to have applied to nos. 16 and 18 as well.

Window VIII.

1 Peter and Paul absolve penitents.

2 The Debtor forgiven by his Lord.

3 Christ forgives believers.

4 Stephen stoned.

5 The Debtor beats his fellow servant.

6 Paul stoned.

7 The wicked sent to Hell-fire.

8 The Debtor given to the tormentors.

9 The Jews slaughtered (? by the Romans).

10 Isaiah preaching.

11 The King sends out servants to invite guests.

12 John (Baptist) preaching.

13 Some follow a king: some flee.

14 Those invited excuse themselves.

15 Peter preaches: they follow Moses and the synagogue.

16 The dead arise.

17 The King visits the guests.

18 The Blessed are called by Christ.

19 Jesus casts the traders out of the temple.

20 The Man without a wedding garment is cast out.

21 Ananias and Sapphira die.

Window IX.

2 Creation of Adam.	1 The Traveller falls among thieves.	[5 Conviction.]
3 Creation of Eve.		6 Expulsion.
4 Fall.		[7 Beginning of Toil.]
9 Moses, Aaron, and Pharaoh.	8 Priest and Levite pass him by.	12 The Law Given.
10 *Tau* written on the lintel.		13 The Golden Calf.
		14 The Brazen Serpent.
11 The Exodus.		
16 The Betrayal.	15 The Samaritan takes him to the Inn.	19 The Entombment.
17 The Scourging (?).		20 The Resurrection.
18 The Crucifixion.		21 The angel and the women.
22 The Holy Spirit between God and Man.	23 Jesus sends disciples to fetch the ass.	24 Jesus between Peter and Paul.
25 Peter brings the Jewish (?) Church.	26 The disciples bring the ass and foal.	27 Paul brings the Gentile (?) Church.
28 Isaiah (Zechariah) with scroll: *Behold thy King cometh,* etc.	29 Jesus riding on the ass, met by children.	30 David with scroll: *Out of the mouths of babes,* etc.

There are several doubtful points here. The subjects of the *Conviction* and *Beginning of Toil* seem indicated in the verses, but not in the titles of the Roll. Perhaps the first scene of the Parable may have had only four types. If so, the *Fall* should be transferred to the right-hand side.

No. 17. The Scourging. In the Roll there is here a title *The maid accusing Peter:* but there is no allusion to this in the verses where the scourging is mentioned.

It is doubtful to me whether nos. 22—30 do really belong to this window. The Parable of the Good Samaritan would amply suffice to fill the whole space, and usually does so in the instances I have seen.

Window X.

1 Abigail meets David.	2 Jairus' daughter raised.	3 Constantine dissuaded from slaughtering children.
4 Penitence of Solomon.	5 The widow's son at Nain raised.	6 Penitence of Theophilus.
7 Jonah before Nineveh.	8 Lazarus raised.	9 Penitence of St Mary of Egypt.

I have already noted that the three raisings from the dead were held to typify three stages of sin.

Window XI.

1 David bearing himself in his hands.	2 The Last Supper.	3 The Manna.
4 Laban washes the camels' feet.	5 Jesus washes the Apostles' feet.	6 Abraham washes the angels' feet.
7 Joseph sold.	8 The Betrayal.	9 Joab slays Abner (Amasa).
10 Job smitten with boils.	11 The Scourging.	12 Elisha mocked.

Window XII.

1 Isaac bearing the wood.	2 Jesus bearing the Cross.	3 The widow of Zarephath with the two sticks.
4 The Brazen Serpent.	5 Jesus nailed to the Cross.	6 The Red Heifer.
8 Death of Abel.	7 The Deposition.	10 Moses sprinkles blood on the lintel.
9 Elisha raises the Shunammite's son.		11 The foreheads of the righteous marked with *Tau* (Ezek. ix.).
12 Samson in Gaza.	13 The Entombment.	14 Jonah swallowed by the fish.

16 David rescues the lamb.

17 Samson carries away the gates.

15 The Harrowing of Hell.

18 Samson rends the lion.

19 Daniel kills the dragon (*Bel and Dragon*).

20 Jonah cast up by the fish.

23 The lion revives his cub.

21 The Resurrection.

24 The Angel and the women.

22 David let down from the window.

25 Joseph released from prison.

26 St Gregory washes the hands of the poor. Christ appears to him.

28 The Host changed into the form of a finger.

27 St Gregory dictates. Peter the deacon writes the Hermit and his cat.

29 St Gregory made Pope against his will.

Possibly no. 26 and no. 27 should be counted as two medallions each.

From the titles as given in the Roll nos. 10 and 11 might be taken as one subject. The verses, however, make it quite clear that two subjects were represented.

The present position of the extant remains of these twelve windows has been already indicated: but it will be worth while to devote rather more space to them. In the first place I should like to make a retractation on my own account. I have more than once in print cited the fact that of the twelve windows only so much survives as to fill two windows now, as a sample of the dreadful neglect and vandalism of the eighteenth century: for I had supposed that the series was still entire when Somner, and even Battely, wrote. This is a complete mistake. Somner, Battely, and every one else who has printed the account of the twelve windows, has been directly or indirectly dependent upon the Roll. In the time of Gostling, whose long life covered the period of greatest neglect (the last quarter of the eighteenth and first quarter of the nineteenth century), no more of this glass was existing than exists now. Gostling's description of it, represented in the *Notes* already mentioned, is a remarkably minute and accurate one, and enables us to check the condition of the glass in his day very satisfactorily. It is of course more than probable that there was neglect and even some amount of destruction under the early Georges: but it is clear that the loss of the greater part of the windows is not due to that but to wilful breakage, perpetrated, I suppose, by Culmer and other such-like brutes during the Cromwellian period.

In the next place I will put out in tabular form a statement of the position of the existing fragments of the glass, which now fill two windows in the north aisle of the choir. Diagrams of them, and illustrations of some portions, are to be found in the *Notes*.

Window B¹.

1 Half-circle.
    Balaam. II. 1.

2 Square.
    The Three Kings journeying. II. 2.

3 Half-circle.
    Isaiah and Jerusalem. II. 3.

4 Square.
    The Pillar of Fire. II. 4.

5 Circle.
    Herod and the Kings. II. 5.

6 Square.
    Christ and the Gentiles. II. 6.

7 Circle.
    Solomon and the Queen of Sheba. II. 7.

8 Square.
    Adoration of the Magi. II. 8.

9 Circle.
    Joseph, his brethren, and the Egyptians. II. 9.

10 Square.
    Lot and Sodom. II. 10.

11 Circle.
    The Magi warned. II. 11.

12 Square.
    Jeroboam and the Prophet. II. 12.

13 Circle.
    Samuel presented. II. 13.

14 Square.
    Presentation of Christ. II. 14.

15 Square.
    Pharisees depart from Christ. VI. 6.

16 Square.
    The Three Estates. VI. 12.

17 Circle.
    Noah, David and Job. VI. 9.

18 Square.
    The Three Sons of Noah. VI. 10.

19 Square.
    The Sower: the Thorns. VI. 8.

20 Right portion of circle.
    The Rich of this world. VI. 7.

21 Circle.
    The Sower: the Birds, etc. VI. 5.

Nos. 1—14 are *in situ*. The remaining subjects are all from window VI.

¹ See the plan, p. 39.

Window C[1].

2 Circle.
Jesus and the
Doctors. III. 2.

1 Half-circle.
Moses and Jethro.
III. 1.

3 Half-circle.
Daniel and the
Elders. III. 3.

5 Circle.
The Apostles fish-
ing. IV. 8.

4 Half-circle.
Noah in the Ark.
III. 4.

6 Half-circle.
The Six Ages of
Man. IV. 6.

8 Circle.
The Miracle of
Cana. IV. 5.

7 Half-circle.
The Six Ages of
the World. IV.
4.

9 Half-circle.
Peter ·and the
Jewish
Church. IV.7.

11 Circle.
Call of Nathanael.
IV. 2.

10 Quarter-circle.
The Pharisees turn
away. VI. 3.

12 Quarter-circle.
The Gentiles seek
the Gospel.
VI. 1.

Nos. 1—4 are *in situ*. The interstices between the circles
and half-circles are filled with small circular medallions not
containing pictures.

Of windows I., V., VII.—XII. no remains exist.

THE POSITION OF THE WINDOWS.

Can we determine the position of the whole series?

At one time I thought that this was possible and, indeed,
an accomplished fact; but a recent visit to Canterbury has
shown me that my hypothetical arrangement was an impossible one, and has filled me with doubts as to the possibility
of discovering the truth. The nature of my difficulties will
appear as I proceed.

There are one or two points which may be regarded, as
established. The first is that the series begins at the west
end of the north aisle of the choir. This is in agreement

[1] See the plan, p. 39.

with the title of the Roll (now, as I conjecture, cut off, but pretty certainly genuine), which runs thus:

" The windows in the upper part of Christ Church, Canterbury, beginning on the north side."

It is borne out by the presence of portions of glass, evidently *in situ*, in the two windows which have just been described.

Secondly, it is fairly evident that all the twelve windows must be looked for in the lower story. Glass of so minute and elaborate a kind as that with which we are dealing must have been placed as near the level of the eye as possible.

Thirdly, the field of our research is bounded on the east and on the west. On the west by the great transept which cannot possibly come into consideration; on the east by the Trinity chapel. Large portions of the original glass exist in the windows of this part of the church. It is of a date not far removed from that of the twelve windows, and, with the exception of two windows in the *Corona*, illustrates the life and miracles of St Thomas of Canterbury.

The following portions of the building, then, are open to us. The north and south choir aisles, the eastern transept, and perhaps a bay on each side eastward of this. In this portion are the following windows.

In the north choir aisle, three, the westernmost blocked (A, B, C)

In the N.E. transept,   one in the west wall (D)

    „   „   two in the north wall (E, F)

    „   „   two in the east wall (G, H)

East of this, one window in the north wall (I)

On the south side

East of the S.E. transept, one window in the south wall (K)

In the S.E. transept,   two in the east wall (L, M)

    „   „   two in the south wall (N, O)

    „   „   one in the west wall (P)

In the south choir aisle three (Q, R, S)

In all, eighteen windows.

From this list we may at once strike out the four windows in the east walls of N.E. and S.E. transept (G, H, L, M). They are too narrow and short for our requirements, and from

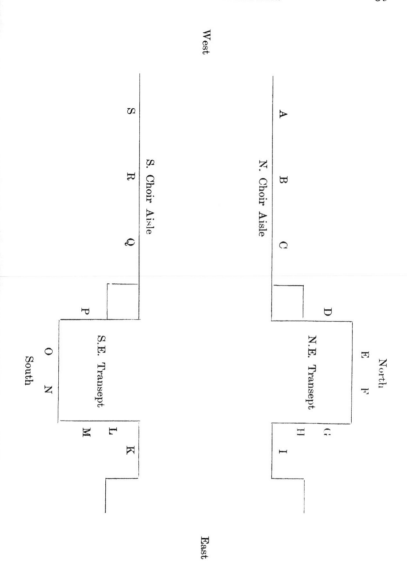

Key-plan of a portion of the Choir of Canterbury Cathedral.
The letters of the alphabet indicate windows.

analogy, and also from fragments of old glass still remaining in one, I conjecture that they illustrated the deeds of the Saints to whom the altars below them were dedicated. Fourteen windows are thus left, and we have glass for twelve of them.

As to the positions of the first six I have really no doubt at all. They are the three windows in the north choir aisle, and those in the west and north walls of the N.E. transept.

We will take these windows singly.

I.   The window A, westernmost in the north choir aisle, has now no glass in it. Gostling tells us that it was blocked up to make room for the staircase to the organ-loft, which, as Dart's view shows, was once above the stalls on the north side. The glass is said to have been destroyed in 1642, and Gostling speaks of the "lead-work" as being visible in his time. It is not to be seen now.

The window contained only 12 subjects in four groups of three each. It is too narrow to allow of their having been arranged in horizontal rows. The side-subjects must have been rather below the central ones. The window Q in the south choir aisle gives an idea of the probable disposition.

2.   The second window, B, has a large portion (14 subjects) of its glass *in situ*. There were originally 21 subjects in seven rows of three. Each row consisted alternately of a square between two circles and a circle between two squares. All the compartments in the iron-work are rectangular. The circular pictures had spandrels of decorative work.

3.   The third window, C, had 12 subjects, of which the first four are *in situ*. The central column of pictures consisted of circles, the lateral ones of half-circles rather below the central ones, on each side. The interstices, as I have said, were filled with small decorative medallions.

4.   The fourth window had 18 subjects, of which six are now in window C. They consisted of half-circles and circles, and were of the same dimensions as those of window C. The window (D) in the west wall of the N.E. transept suits these conditions exactly. Its iron-work is apparently original.

5. Of the glass of the fifth window no remains exist. It had 16 subjects : in one case I conjecture that one medallion contained two scenes. There would, according to my notion, have been four groups of these subjects, and two groups of two. The westernmost window (E) in the N. wall of the N.E. transept has iron-work which points to three groups, each of four subjects surrounding a central circle.

6. The sixth window contained 18 subjects, nine of which are now in existence, seven of them being in window B, and two in window C. Two are quarter-circles, four are squares, and three are or have been complete circles. The general arrangement evidently resembled that of window B. The window F, easternmost in the west wall of the N.E. transept, contains iron-work for 18 subjects, all rectangular : so that, as in window B, the circular subjects must have been filled out into squares by spandrels of ornament.

Of the remaining six windows no fragment now exists : and the iron-work does not help me towards ascertaining their positions. We have the following *data* to satisfy.

The seventh window had 18 subjects in sets of three.

The eighth window, 21 subjects in sets of three.

The ninth, 28 subjects : three groups of either five or seven and three groups of three. The window K, east of the S.E. transept, would perhaps have contained the first three groups.

I am inclined to suspect that the scribe of the Roll has been careless here, and has mixed two windows up together, the Good Samaritan and the Entry into Jerusalem. Perhaps the last nine subjects of no. IX. may really have been in no. X., which is described as containing only nine subjects in sets of three.

The eleventh window had 12 subjects in sets of three. This suits well enough with the iron-work of window Q, west of the S.E. transept.

The twelfth window had, according to the Roll, no less than 30 subjects. The first 25 seem to have been partly in sets of three, partly in sets of five. These were followed by either four or six scenes from the life of St Gregory, which are pretty clearly only a fragment of a larger window[1].

I can find no window in that part of the Cathedral which is open to us large enough to have contained all the glass. The one that approaches the required dimensions most nearly is R, immediately opposite to B, and of the same size. Its present iron-work is like that of B, but seems modern.

The windows in the south and west wall of the S.E. transept (N, O, P) have elaborate iron-work which may be modern, and which in any case will not accommodate the glass of any of the windows in the Roll. The same may be said of window S in the south choir aisle, which corresponds in size and position to A, and at present contains three groups of five subjects in modern glass.

To sum up : windows I.—VI. in the Roll correspond with windows A—F on the plan. Windows XI. and XII. may very probably be equated with Q and R. For the rest I can at present find no place.

I cannot help suspecting that a thirteenth window must have been at least designed, if it was never executed. It is needed to bring the series to the proper and customary conclusion. In it the chain of events would have been carried on through the appearances of our Lord after the Resurrection (especially those to Mary Magdalene, to Thomas, and to the disciples at Emmaus); it would have continued with the Ascension, and would have ended with the Descent of the Holy Ghost, or perhaps with the Last Judgment. Such a window might very fittingly have been placed westernmost in the south aisle of the choir, corresponding in position to no. I. on the north side.

---

[1] They may very possibly have been transferred from window M (E. wall of S.E. transept), below which was an altar of St Gregory.

NOTES

THE PAINTED GLASS

IN

CANTERBURY CATHEDRAL

WITH A PREFACE

BY THE

VERY REV. F. W. FARRAR, D.D., F.R.S.

DEAN OF CANTERBURY

All Proceeds towards the Cathedral Restoration Fund

ABERDEEN UNIVERSITY PRESS

1897

PREFACE.

In the following valuable but unpretending pages, I believe that every reader will find a more convenient guide than has yet been published to the study of the old stained glass windows in Canterbury Cathedral. It need hardly be said that the more ancient windows contain some of the finest thirteenth century glass in England ; and it is at least probable that there are fragments of stained glass still remaining in them which are even older. When Richard Culmer, the fanatical Rector of Chartham, occupied himself in " rattling down proud Becket's glassy bones," he ruined in a few hours the work of years, and ignorantly inflicted upon the Cathedral an amount of damage which can never be repaired. Fortunately, however, his career of furious iconoclasm was checked before he had utterly destroyed the entire series of those

" Storied windows richly dight
   Shedding a dim religious light,"

which would now have been of priceless value. But the windows, and parts of windows, which escaped the pikes of the Puritans are precious from their connection with the progress of a beautiful art, of which the secrets are partly lost, and because of the intensely interesting light which they throw upon the history, the legends and the religious beliefs of the Middle Ages. A little has been done of late years to gather together these scattered fragments of glass which once presented continuous scenes from the miraculous interventions of Archbishop Becket, as told by Monkish chroniclers. But without the help of such a

book as this the ordinary visitor to the Cathedral would
find himself hopelessly unable to decipher the meaning of
pictures of which the continuity has been repeatedly dis-
turbed, and of which the Latin rhyming descriptions are
often too confused to be any longer intelligible.   The
preparation of these pages has been a labour of love on
the part of the author.   She has conferred a real obligation
on all who love Canterbury Cathedral, and who desire to
learn something more from its records and memories than
can be acquired by a rapid and superficial glance at its
outward appearance.   Had such monographs as this been
more common, we should be in possession of many interesting details now lost in oblivion, and England would
perhaps show a deeper interest in her glorious Cathedrals,
and a more munificent desire to save them from an im-
poverishment which cripples their resources and a decay
which in time will spoil their beauty.   I hope that this
little book may be so heartily welcomed as to encourage
future efforts in a similar direction, and gradually to fulfil
the poet's aspiration :—

" Wake again, Teutonic Father-ages,
   Speak again, beloved primæval creeds ;
Flash ancestral spirit from your pages,
   Wake the greedy age to nobler deeds.
           .   .   .   .
" Old decays but foster new creations ;
   Bones and ashes feed the golden corn ;
Fresh elixirs wander every moment
   Down the veins through which the live past feeds its child, the
      live unborn."

                                        F. W. FARRAR.
      21st May, 1897.

THE aim of these very imperfect notes is to give some account of
the changes which have taken place in the arrangement of the old
painted glass, and to keep a distinct record of modern additions.

TABLE OF CONTENTS.

		PAGE
1. THE CLERESTORY		1
2. WINDOWS IN THE NORTH AISLE OF CHOIR...		4
3. NORTH AND SOUTH TRIFORIUM		15
4. NORTH AND SOUTH CHOIR TRANSEPTS		21
5a. TRINITY CHAPEL AND BECKET'S CROWN		21
5b. TRINITY CHAPEL		29
6. SOUTH TRANSEPT OF NAVE		44
7. WEST WINDOW IN THE NAVE...		46
8. NORTH TRANSEPT OF NAVE		48
9. THE DEAN'S CHAPEL AND S. MICHAEL'S		51
10. THEOLOGICAL WINDOWS		52
11. STORIES TRANSLATED FROM THE LATIN CHRONICLES		64
12. MODERN WINDOWS		72

PLATES.

NORTH TRANSEPT OF CHOIR.

PAGE

1. The Conversion of the Heathen 7
2. The Church and Noe's Sons 10
3. The Marriage in Cana 14
4. The Calling of Nathanael 14

NORTH TRIFORIUM.

5. The Forester 15
6. The Siege of Canterbury 17
7. The Taking of S. Alphege 17
8. The Murder of the Monks 17

SOUTH TRIFORIUM.

9. William of Kellett 18
10. The Tomb in the Crypt 23
11. On the Altar 35

TRINITY CHAPEL—SOUTH SIDE—WINDOW VI.

12. The Fever 41
13. The Offering 41
14. The Fall of the Wall 41
15. The Mother Faints 41
16. The Deliverance 42
17. The Offering at the Tomb 43
18. A Cripple at the Tomb 43
19. A Leper Priest 43
20. The Fall of Earth on William of Gloucester 43
21. Two Men Bring the News that he is Dead 43
22. A Dismal Groan is Heard 43
23. The Good News is Told 43
24. Men Arrive with Country Tools 43
25. William is Brought Out 43
26. A Lady Offering a Coil 43
27. A Lady Kneeling at an Altar 43

PLANS.

		PAGE
1.	THE CHOIR	2
2.	WINDOW IN NORTH AISLE OF CHOIR	6
3.	WINDOW IN NORTH AISLE OF CHOIR	12
4.	WINDOW IN NORTH TRIFORIUM (WEST)	16
5.	WINDOW IN NORTH TRIFORIUM (CENTRE)	16
6.	WINDOW IN NORTH TRIFORIUM (EAST)	17
7.	WINDOW IN SOUTH TRIFORIUM (EAST)	18
8.	WINDOW IN SOUTH TRIFORIUM (CENTRE)	19
9.	WINDOW IN SOUTH TRIFORIUM (WEST)	20
10.	WINDOW IN BECKET'S CROWN	26
11.	THIRD WINDOW IN TRINITY CHAPEL (NORTH)	28
12.	FOURTH WINDOW IN TRINITY CHAPEL (NORTH)	30
13.	FIFTH WINDOW IN TRINITY CHAPEL (NORTH)	33
14.	SIXTH WINDOW IN TRINITY CHAPEL (NORTH)	36
15.	FIRST WINDOW, SOUTH SIDE	40
16.	FIFTH WINDOW, SOUTH SIDE	40
17.	SIXTH WINDOW, SOUTH SIDE	42
18.	ORIGINAL WINDOW BOTH IN NORTH AND SOUTH CHOIR TRANSEPTS	42
19.	ADAPTED TO THIS PLAN	42
20.	WINDOW IN SOUTH TRANSEPT OF NAVE	44
21.	WEST WINDOW IN THE NAVE	47
22.	WINDOW IN THE NORTH TRANSEPT	48

The plans are (approximately) to the scale of ¼ inch to a foot. The last three excepted.

b

AUTHORITIES.

The Antiquities of Canterbury, by W. Somner, 1640 ; 1st edition.

Cathedrall Newes from Canterbury, recorded and published by Richard Culmer, 1644.

History and Antiquities of the Cathedral Church of Canterbury, by the Rev. Mr. J. Dart, 1726.

Description of the Cathedral of Christ Church, by John Barnby, solicitor, 1772.

History of Kent, by Edward Hasted, 1788-1790 ; vol. iv., 1799.

Twelve Perspective Views of the Metropolitical Church of Canterbury, by Charles Wild, 1807.

A Walk in and about the City of Canterbury, by W. Gostling ; new edition, 1825.

Heraldic Notices of Canterbury Cathedral, by Thomas Willement, 1827.   Harding Lepard.

Canterbury in the Olden Time, by Felix Summerley (Sir H. Cole), 1860.

Historical Memorials of Canterbury, by Dean Stanley.   Murray.

Materials for the History of Thomas Becket, edited by J. C. Robertson, M.A., Canon of Canterbury, 1875.   Will. I. refers to William of Canterbury ;   Bened. II. refers to Benedict of Canterbury.

Arch. Journal, 1876.   Early Glass in Canterbury Cathedral, by W. J. Loftie, B.A.

History of Design in Painted Glass, by N. H. J. Westlake, F.S.A. Parker, 1879.

The Crypt of Canterbury Cathedral, by W. A. Scott-Robertson, M.A., Hon. Canon of Canterbury.   Mitchell & Hughes, 1880.

Chronological Conspectus, by the same.   Arch. Cant., vol. xiv.

NOTES ON THE PAINTED GLASS

IN

CANTERBURY CATHEDRAL.

THE CLERESTORY.

THIRTY-THREE of the forty-nine windows are copies, by the late Mr. George Austin,[1] of the glass formerly there. The subjects represented the ancestry of our Lord, beginning on the north side of the choir with the Almighty and Adam, passing round both transepts, and ending with our Lord and the Blessed Virgin. Two figures, one above the other, are in each window, those to the east being smaller and in medallions.

Mr. Westlake draws attention to their very close resemblance in all particulars to those in the lancet windows at Chartres and in the Abbey of S. Rémi at Rheims, and he is convinced that they were designed in the same school. No record has been discovered of the exact place, but it is his belief that the designs originated from an atelier at Chartres or its neighbourhood, though whether executed there or in England it is impossible to say.[2]

Some windows must have been among the "window images" demolished in 1642.

[1] See XIII. "Modern Windows."

[2] Mr. Westlake, who has kindly looked over these notes, remarks: "I am inclined to say that the clerestory windows were the oldest in the Cathedral. Those that are still there may be a little after 1200. The style is between those at S. Rémi and those at Chartres. No window is entirely in the style of the twelfth century, although earlier details enter into all thirteenth century work."

25 — EAST.

The Ascension. The Crucifixion. The Nativity.

24 — Transfiguration. The Agony. The Magi.

26 — The Resurrection. Flagellation. Flight into Egypt.

23 — Moses striking the Rock. Giving the Law.

27 — Baptism. Beheading S. John Baptist.

No.	Names
2	Seth. Enos.
3	Cainan. Malaleel.
4	Jared. Enoch.
5	Methusaleh. Lamech.
6	Noe. Sem.
7	Arphaxad. Cainan.
8	Sala. Heber.
10	Phalec. Ragan.
11	Saruch. Nachor.
12	Thare. Abram.
13	Isaac. Jacob, now Shem.
14	Juda. Phares.
15	Esrom. Aram.
16	Aminadab. Naason.
17	Salmon. Booz.
18	Obed. Jesse.
19	David. Nathan.
20	Roboas. Abias.
21	Ezechias. Josias.
22	Jeconias. Salathiel.
28	Mattatha. Menan.
29	Melea. Eliakim.
30	Jonan. Joseph.
31	Jude. Simeon.
32	Levi. Matthat.
33	Jorim. Eliezer.
34	Jose. Sher.
35	Elmodam. Cosam.
36	Addi. Melchi.
37	Neri. Salathiel, now Esaias.
38	Zorobabel. Rhesa.
39	Joanna. Juda.
40	Joseph. Semei.
42	Mattathias. Maath.
43	Nagge. Esli.
44	Naum. Amos.
45	Mattatha. Joseph.
46	Janna. Melchior.
47	Levi. Matthat.
48	Heli. Joseph. B. V. Mary.

NORTH TRANSEPT. 6, 7, 8, 9, 11, 12 now blank.

SOUTH TRANSEPT. 38, 39, 40, 42, 43, 44 now blank.

About 1779 the lower part of the first window in the clerestory is spoken of as "quite defaced, having been a design to represent the Almighty, and several of the rest are without figures ".[1]

"Some with carpet patterns of the most beautiful colours, but where any are remaining the style in which they are drawn, and the thrones on which they are placed, much resemble those of the kings on the reverse of their earliest royal seals." [2]

In 1799 the window in the south transept of the nave " was selected and arranged with much care and industry by Mr. John Simmonds, one of the vesturers of the church, to whom the arrangement was committed by the Dean and Chapter ".[3]

Some of the clerestory figures were placed there, and some in the west window of the nave, " and some glass was sold to a connoisseur ".[4]

The fragments that were purchased by the connoisseur came into the possession of the late Mr. George Austin, who, in 1861-2, replaced what he could and refilled the clerestory windows with copies of the old, arranging them according to their former position as shown by Gostling.[5]

The plan is of the choir and windows to which the figures have been removed. The numbers show the original position in the clerestory, corresponding with their present places in the nave and south transept. Two original figures still remain. The upper figure of No. 13, Shem, in the south transept, removed from No. 6 ; and the lower figure, Esaias, No. 37, in the south. The latter is similar to one at Chartres. The head, cap, hands and part of the drapery are new, but copied by Mr. Caldwell from the old, which was falling to pieces.

At the east end part of the chequer work is old in

---

[1] Barnby.   [2] Hasted, iv., 529.   [3] *Ibid.*, iv., 521.
[4] *Chronological History of Canterbury Cathedral*, 381.
[5] *Handbook of Canterbury*, by Felix Summerley.

Nos. 24, 25, 26 (in parts). The old borders remain in Nos. 1, 4, 5, 6, 12, 13, 14, 17, 20, 24 (in part), 25, 26, 33 (in part), 34, 36, 37, 38.

Possibly the chequer work surrounding the two Becket subjects in the south transept came from here.

Note from a MS. by Mr. G. Austin, from whom the arrangement of windows is copied :—

" The names mentioned in Gostling's list of windows, Nos. 20, 21, 22, are part of the pedigree given by S. Matthew, but all the others are according to a pedigree given by S. Luke, who, writing for the Gentiles, traced the pedigree through our Lord's Mother to David. Were these names introduced to fill up the extra number of windows? The pedigree, as given by S. Luke, including the Virgin, would contain seventy-eight names, requiring thirty-nine windows. But there are forty-seven in the clerestory. But (Nos. 23, 24, 25, 26, 27) five of them have been filled with medallions, thus leaving forty-two, being three more than S. Luke's pedigree would fill. Query —If six names from S. Matthew's pedigree were interpolated to fill up the range?

" No. 33. These figures must have been in No. 28 (Gostling). They were probably moved, as No. 33 is most seen from the choir. No. 28 cannot be seen " (Mr. G. Austin).

THE TWO WINDOWS IN THE NORTH AISLE OF CHOIR.

There were originally twelve windows with scriptural subjects, each subject being illustrated by types and their fulfilment, with an explanatory legend surrounding each.

A description of the windows is in a MS. in the library of Corpus Christi College at Oxford, folio 185, which Mr. Coxe considered to be of the sixteenth or seventeenth century. It is copied in Somner's *Antiquities* and in other works. The subjects, according to Mr. Winston, were arranged three in a row, the main subject in the centre and a type on either side, like those represented in the *Biblia Pauperum*. An exact date of the glass has not been ascertained. Mr. Loftie[1] puts it at about 1174, from a comparison of similar pictures in a MS. book of pictures in the British Museum, written for the nuns at Shaftesbury. But Mr. Westlake[2] ascribes the glass to the first half of the thirteenth century.

The organ formerly stood above these windows as it is represented in Dart, though not quite correctly. The first window of the twelve was then blocked up to make room for the staircase, the marks of which are quite plain. The leading of the window is still there, but the glass, which chiefly related to the Virgin Mary, was destroyed in 1642. The position of the remaining nine windows of the twelve is not known.

Window I., Formerly II.

Fourteen of these medallions were always here, and seven are from the window described as VI. in the Oxford MS. The Roman figures in the centre of the circles refer to the window from which the medallion was taken.[3] The central subjects represented events in the life of our Lord, the types being on either side.

The description of these windows is from *A Walk in Canterbury*, by William Gostling, Minor Canon.

I.—1. Balaam riding on an Ass.

Over him is Balaam. The inscription round it is—

ORIETUR STELLA EX JACOB ET CONSURGET
VIRGO DE ISRAEL.

---

[1] Loftie, *Archæological Journal.*
[2] Westlake, vol. i., 104.
[3] Copies of those contained in this window are in one by Mr. G. Austin in the north transept of choir.

2. The Three Wise Men riding.

They seem to be in doubt of the way.   Over them the star.   No inscription.[1]

3. The Prophet Isaiah standing near a gate leading into the City.

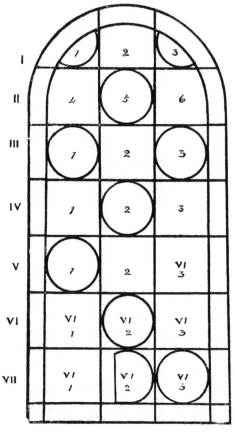

PLAN 2.

By his head YSA.   The inscription is—
AMBVLABVNT GENTES IN LUMINE TVO ET REGES IN SPLENDORE ORT, BENIAM.

[1] Very similar to the Magi represented in a MS. book of pictures, *Nero*, c. iv., British Museum.

THE CONVERSION OF THE HEATHEN.

Plate I.   *Page* 7.

II.—1. Pharaoh and Moses leading the People out of Egypt.

Pharaoh sitting under the entrance into his palace and an Egyptian standing by him. Pharaoh points to Moses, who is at the head of a group of Israelitish men, women and children, conducting them out of Egypt. He holds his rod in his left hand and points to the sea before them with his right. In the air before them is the miraculous pillar. Over Pharaoh is—

PHARAO REX EGYPTI.

Over the Israelites—

ISRL SEQUENS COLVMPNAM.

Over is—

EXIT ABERVMPNA POPVLUS DVCENTE COL-
VMPNA.

Under is—

STELLA MAGOS DUXIT LVX XPS VTRISQ
RELVXIT.

2. Herod and the Wise Men.

Herod sitting in a pensive attitude receives the account of the three wise men, who are standing before him. Over their heads is the star, and under them TRES MAGI. Over Herod, HERODES. Behind his chair stands a person with his right hand expanded as if in astonishment. No inscription.

3. The Conversion of the Heathens.

The heathens turning their backs on an idol temple (in which is an idol standing upon a pillar) follow Christ, who is going up a staircase leading into a Christian temple, within which is a golden cross standing upon an altar, and before which on the ground is a baptismal font.

Over is—

STELLA MAGOS DVXIT. ET EOS AB HERODE
REDVXIT.

(A star led the wise men and brought them back from Herod.)

Under is—

SIC SATHANAM GENTES FVGIVNT : TE XPE SEQUENTES.[1]

(Thus the Gentiles flee from Satan, following thee, O Christ.)

III.—1. Solomon and the Queen of Sheba.

Solomon on his throne, with attendants, receives the Queen of Sheba, who addresses him standing before him. Her attendants are on horseback.

Under is—

REX SALLOM : REGINA SABA.

Round is—

HIC DONAT DONIS REGINA DOMVM SALO-MINIS.

SIC REGES DOMINO DANT M(VN)ERA TRES TRIATRINO.

2. The Wise Men offering.

The Virgin sits in the middle with the Child in her lap, but has been broken and badly repaired. On one hand are the wise men offering, over whom is the star. On the other side stand the shepherds. No inscription.

3. Joseph and his Brethren.

Joseph sitting in a chair of state receives on one side his suppliant brethren. On the other side stand the Egyptians. Over his head—

JOSEPH.

At the bottom is—

FRS ISOPH ✠ EGIPTI.

In the round—

AD TE LONGI (NQVOS) IOSEPH ATRAHIS ATQ PROPINQVOS.

SIC DEUS IN CUNIS IUDEOS GENTIBUS VNIS.

IV.—1. Lot and Sodom.

The destruction of Sodom. The angel conducting Lot and his two daughters, and his wife looking back.

---

[1] This is in the Latin MS. on Herod and the Magi.

Over is—

VT LOTH SALVETUR NE RESPICIAT BETVR :
PROHI. (Misplaced. For prohibetur.)
SIC VITANT REVEHI : PER HERODIS REGNA
SABET.

2. The Wise Men warned in a Dream.[1]

The angel appearing to the wise men, who are on a bed
sleeping. The angel holds a scroll on which there remains
now only HERODE, the letters SECU before it being a
patch. No inscription.

3. Jeroboam and the Prophet.

Jeroboam sacrificing at an altar, by which stand several
persons, turns to the prophet, who admonishes him.
Over his head is—

REX IEROBOAM.

Behind the prophet is—

PPHETA.

Over is—

UT VIA MVTETVR REDEVNDO : PPHETA MO-
NETVR.

Under is—

SIC TRES EGERVNT : QUI XPO DONA TVLERUNT.

Over the prophet's head is—

NE REDEAS VIA QUA VENISTI.

V.—1. Samuel presented.

Eli in the temple receives Samuel from Hannah. Over
his head HELI SACERDOS. An attendant with the
bullock, flour and wine for the offering.
Round is—

GEMINVM. TRIPLEX. OBLATIO. TRINVM.
SIGNIFICAT. DOMINVM. SAMVEL. PUER.
AMPHORA VINUM.

2. Christ presented.

[1] The same subject is in a window in the Cathedral at Le Mans.
Westlake, vol. i., p. 11. Also in the MS. book of pictures, *Nero*, c. iv.,
British Museum, but one king is sitting up in bed listening to the angel.

Simeon in the temple holds out his hands to receive Christ from the Virgin. An attendant stands behind her with a pair of turtle doves for the offering. No inscription.

3. The Pharisees rejecting Christ.

The Pharisees going away from Christ, who holds a scroll.

NISI (MANDUCA) CAVERITIS CARNEM (FILII HOMINIS).

Over is—

SEMEN RORE CARENS EXPERS RATIONIS ET ARENS.

Under is—

HI SVNT QUI CREDVNT TENTANTVR SICQ. RECE(DUNT).

VI.—1. Virginity, Continence and Matrimony.

Represented by three figures, holding each a scroll with their names inscribed—

VIRGO : CONTINENS : CONIVGATVS.

Over is—

ATA TRIA TRES FRVCTUS OPERATA.

Which belonged to another window now broken.

Under is—

SVNT VXORATIS ET VIRGINIBVS VIDVATIS.

2. The Three Just Men, Daniel, Job and Noah.

Holding each a scroll with their names inscribed— DANIEL : JOB : NOE. Three angels hovering in the air put crowns on their heads.

Round is—

(VERBA P) RIS SE(RVIT DEUS (HIS FRV)CTVS SIBI CREVIT.

In the remainder of this round is a patch.

REPROBANTUR PARS TADO

IN TELLURE BO(NA TRIPLEX : SVA CVIQV CORONA).

3. The Church and Noah's Three Sons.

" IVRIN is inserted instead of ECCLE."

THE CHURCH AND NOE'S SONS.

Plate 2.   *Page* 10.

Over their heads [ECCLE]SIA : SEM : CHEM : JAPHET. The figure representing the church holds a scroll, the characters on which are so placed that they could not be read. Cham holds a circular scroll containing—

PARTE NOE NATI MI(C)HI QVISQ(VE) SVA
    DOMINATI.

(Noah's sons ruling for me, each over his own part.)
Over is—

UNA FIDES NATIS EX HIS TRIBVS EST DEI-
    TATIS.

(From these three sons is one belief in the Deity.)
Under is—

VERIT : ✠ EUM PRO SEODE ABELDESHOBORAT.
(In the three divisions of the world, MUNDVS is inscribed.)

VII.—1. The Sower.

With the thorns growing up.
Over him—

(SEM)INATOR.

2. The Rich Men of this World.

Two figures (between them is written IVLIANVS MAVRITIUS), one crowned, with a vessel of gold heaped up standing before them. The inscription is—

(ISTI SPI) NOSI (LOCVPLETES] DELICIOSI :
NIL FRUCTUS REFERVNT QVONIAM TERRE-
    STRIA [QVERUNT.

3. The Sower and Fowls of the Air.

No inscription.

(The last three stages apparently contained the following subjects :—

V.—1. The Presentation of Samuel.	2. The Presentation of Christ.	3. The Offering of Melchisedek.
2. The Flight of Elijah.	2. The Flight into Egypt.	3. The Flight of David.
3. The Murder of the Benjamites.	3. The Murder of the Innocents.	3. The Murder of the Priests.)

Window II.

(This, the third window, has only four remaining of the original set of medallions, *i.e.*, the first three and Noah in the Ark. The remainder are from the fourth, fifth and sixth windows.)

The pictures in the next window consist of large round pieces, and half-rounds alternately.

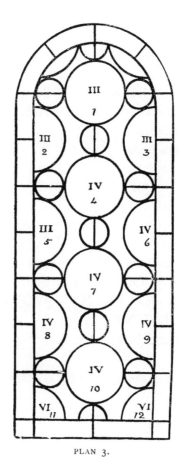

PLAN 3.

1. Jesus among the Doctors.
Under is—

        IHS DVODENNIS IN MEDIO DOCTRUM.
Nothing round.

2. Jethro seeing Moses judging the People.

Moses sitting in a regal chair hears the Israelites who are standing before him.   Jethro stands attentive beside him.
Over Moses—

MOYSES.

Behind Jethro—

JETHRO.

Round is—

SIC HOMINES (AV) DIT I SIC HINC VIR SANCTVS
    OBAV DIT.

GENTILIS VERBIS HVMILES SVNT FORMA SVPER-
    BIS.

3. Daniel among the Elders.
Over him—

DANIEL.

Round is—

MIRANTVR PVERI SENIORES (VOC) E DOCERI.

SIC RES (PONSA DEI SENSVMQ STVPENT
    PHARISEI).

4. The Miraculous Draught of Fishes.
Christ bids the Apostles draw the net into the ship.
Under is—

PISCATIO APLORUM : RETE RVPITVR.

5. Noah receives the Dove bringing the Olive Branch
into the Ark.
Under is—

NOE IN ARCHA.

Round is—

FLVXV CVNCTA VAGO SVBMERGENS PRIMA
    VORAGO.

OMNIA PVRGAVIT BAPTISMAQVE SIGNIFICA-
    VIT.

6. The Six Ages of Man, SEX HOMINIS (ETATES),
represented by as many figures ; over each was his title,
INFANTIA, PUERITIA, ADOLESCENTIA JUVEN-
TUS, VIRILITAS, SENECTUS which was round it has

been rubbed off by injudicious cleaning (as indeed have many words in other parts of the windows), and a fragment of another put with it.

7. The Marriage in Cana.

Jesus at a table with the guests.   In the foreground stand the six water pots with the servant pouring water into them, in allusion to which are formed the allegorical pictures given in Nos. 6 and 8.   (The heads of the three figures to the right are false.   Opposite to the figure of our Lord is a fish on a plate.)

8. The Six Ages of the Church.

Represented by six persons, over whom is written (MUNDI) SEX ETATES.   You must begin with the person at the bottom, and you will find their names as you ascend, in the following order :—

ADAM, NOE, ABRAH, DAVID, JECHONIAS, the name of JESVS, the sixth person, is not written, his figure being everywhere distinguished by three bright spots in the red nimbus surrounding his head.   The inscription round, which has suffered much in cleaning, is—

HYDRIA METRETAS CAPIENS, EST QUELIBET
     ETAS LYMPHA DAT HISTORIAM VINVM
     NOTAT ALLEGORIAM.

9. S. Peter with the Jewish Converts.

Peter sitting.   By him S. PETRVS.   At the bottom sits a female figure, under which is ECCL(ES)IA DE JV-DEIS.   Under a building on one side are the Pharisees going away.   Over them, PHARISEI.
Round is—

VERBVM RETE RATIS PETRI. DOMVS HEC
     PIETATIS: PISCES JVDEI. QVI RETE FERANT:
     PHARISEI.

10. The calling of Nathanael.

This picture consists of two parts.   In one is represented Philip speaking to Nathanael sitting under the fig tree ; over them is respectively, PHILIPP, NATHANAEL, FICUS.

THE MARRIAGE IN CANA.

Plate 3.   *Page* 14.

THE CALLING OF NATHANIEL.

Plate 4.

Page 14.

THE FORESTER.

Plate 5.   Page 15.

In the other is represented JESUS (distinguished by his nimbus) receiving Nathanael, Peter and Andrew standing by. Over them PETRVS, ANDREAS, NATHANAEL. Nathanael holds in his hand a scroll containing UNDE ME NOSTI. In Christ's hand is a scroll broken, and illegible.

11. The Pharisees rejecting the Gospel.

Round is—

HI SVNT VERBA DEI QVI CONTEMNUNT PHARISEI.

Almost rubbed out—

12. The Gentiles seeking the Gospel.

Round is—

SOLICITE GENTES SVNT VERBA DEI SITIENTES.

THE TRIFORIUM (NORTH SIDE).

" The upper range of windows in the western part of both aisles, having been entirely demolished, have since been filled up with fragments from other places, and however beautiful the colours may be, there is no making out what they are intended to represent." [1]

West Window No 1.

These three medallions are not in their original position. The scrolling of the window had to be cut to fit them in here.

1. Is composed of fragments of angel wings, of our Lord in clouds, and of a large figure of a priest.

2. This medallion from its original size and border appears to have belonged to I., South Side of the Trinity Chapel.

It represents the story of Adam, a forester, who had " caught three men who had killed a wild beast. One of

---

[1] Hasted, 2nd ed., 1801, p. 379.

them casting a dart pierced the throat of his assailant," [1] who is falling backwards. His companion holds an axe in one hand. To the right one of the outlaws is walking away with

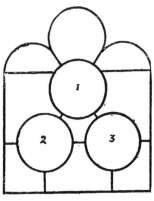

PLAN 4.

the deer slung on a pole over his shoulder. The inscription is : Fur fugiens guttur perforat insequentis. (The fleeing thief pierces the throat of his pursuer.)

3. Was originally a quatrefoil and has been cut to fit in here. It is filled with fragments of angel wings, etc.

CENTRE WINDOW.

In this window is the earliest glass. The scrolling is in its original place.

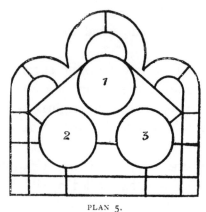

PLAN 5.

[1] Will. I., 342.

THE SIEGE OF CANTERBURY.

Plate 6.   Page 17.

THE TAKING OF S. ALPHEGE.

Plate 7.

Page 17.

THE MURDER OF THE MONKS.

Plate 8.   *Page 17.*

1. Is filled with fragments.

2. The siege of Canterbury by the Danes. From the castle wall two knights are piercing the enemy with their lances and two are hurling stones. On either side of the entrance are also four knights doing the same; only part of the one to the right has gone.

3. Removed from another window. This was originally a quatrefoil, fragments of crowns, a ruby nimbus and hand, and great white star.

Third Window.

Part of the border and scrolling in their original place.

1. The remains of a figure seated on a throne. Another figure approaches with hands extended.

2. In its original place, but it ought to be turned round to the right.

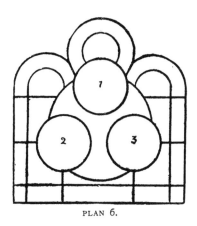

PLAN 6.

Archbishop Alphege is being taken on board the Danish vessel by a knight holding his right arm, and by another pushing him from behind.

3. Fragments of the murder of the monks and apparently of the Archbishop. The head has gone, but a mitre and part of the pall remain.

2

TRIFORIUM (SOUTH SIDE).

The three windows on this side were restored by Mr. Caldwell about 1866 by the order of Dean Alfred.

WINDOW I.

Is probably from a window in the Trinity Chapel, perhaps the first on the south side. It and five other medallions belong to the story of William of Kellett, the wounded carpenter.[1] Borders have been added to make them fit. The story relates how William had vowed to go to the shrine of S. Thomas, but had neglected to do so. He had, however, in shutting up his house in the morning, made the sign of the Cross on his forehead, and commended him-

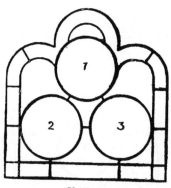

PLAN 7.

self to the saint's protection. When at work, his hand slipped " and the steel of the axe buried itself in his shin ". Fortunately the saint remembering his morning prayer, forgives and heals him. The way in which the story should be read is as follows : III.—1. He is wounded. I.—1. He is being bandaged. II.—2. He has a vision. I.—3. He recovers. II.—1. He makes an offering. II.—3. He joyfully leaves the city.

1. The leg is being bandaged by a woman, part of whose drapery is new. Inscription : Ligaturam solvit vulnus non

[1] Will. I., 273.

M OPATVR NVAMSE(NFTOGROTT

WILLIAM OF KELLETT.

Plate 9.   *Page* 18.

repperit (perhaps, solvit linteolum, vuluus non repperit ullam). He loosed the linen cloth, he did not find any wound.

2. Possibly the story of John of Roxburgh,[1] the first part being in III.—3. He was thrown from his horse into the Tweed. With the saint's help, he reached the toll-keeper's cottage on the bridge, when he suddenly sank down deprived of sight and hearing. He is represented lying with closed eyes on his white cloak, the toll-keeper's wife holding up one of his arms. A great fire is lit. The smoke is new, but copied from a fragment, probably from the fifth window, south side, in the Trinity Chapel. There are no less than seven borders, three being added.[2]

3. Represents William of Kellett sitting up in bed and drinking. All the heads are new, and much of the rest.

WINDOW II.

1. William is kneeling before the altar with its relics. All the figures, excepting the left-hand one, are new.

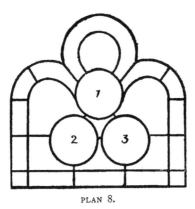

PLAN 8.

[1] Will. I., 296.

[2] With regard to the difficulty of identifying the stories related in the chronicles, Mr. Westlake remarks that "variations constantly occur in mediæval repetition of events related to the artist". The stories of the miracles being unknown in later days, heads and figures are often intro-duced to supply deficiencies with no connection. In the same way the inscriptions are sometimes treated and shifted from one medallion to another. Letters of various alphabets which may happen to fit are inserted, and sometimes upside down.

2. William is rewarded for saying, " Let not mortal aid be sought.   I commit the whole case to the Lord and to the martyr, Thomas."   The saint appears to him in a dream, and he is healed, and says, " Loose my leg, I am whole ".   Much of this medallion is new, but the figure of William is original.

3. He is leaving the city after his cure, with his axe in his hand.   The city is partly new.   Part of the ruby scrolling on the right is from the second window, north side, Trinity Chapel.   It was cut up to fit in here.   Some of the scrolling is taken from the sixth window on the south side of Trinity Chapel.

WINDOW III.

With the exception of the lowest part, the border is the same as in II.   The right and left shoulders have been partly cut out of other windows.

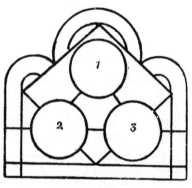

PLAN 9.

1. Represents William with the axe which has just slipped and cut his leg.

2. Is from another window, perhaps the fifth, south side, Trinity Chapel.   A boy sitting up on a bed, resting on a bier covered by a pall.   The heads and part of the drapery new.   Perhaps the story of Philip Scot, who was drowned while stoning a frog as it came out of the swamp.[1]

[1] Will. I., 200.

The inscription may be—

Dat vires sanctus vertunt in gaudia planctus. (The saint gives strength, lamentations are changed to rejoicings.)

3. May be the first part of the story of John of Roxburgh. The horse is being pulled by the bridle out of the water.

THE NORTH AND SOUTH TRANSEPTS OF THE CHOIR.

In the north transept are the remains of a very beautiful rose window. The two central subjects represent Moses (left) holding the Tables of the Law, and a figure representing the Synagogue holding the Levitical books. Around are the cardinal virtues. Justice with a pair of scales stooping over a bag of gold, and on either side, Prudence with two birds, and Temperance with a cup and lighted torch. At the base is Fortitude slaying a serpent. Around are Isaiah, Jeremiah, Ezekiel and Daniel. Probably the minor prophets were in the outer circle. The heads of Moses and the Synagogue were replaced about 1859.[1]

THE SOUTH TRANSEPT.

The late Mr. George Austin made the present arrangement in modern glass, calling the window the new Church. The Apostles, Evangelists and virtues are represented in imitation of the old, and pronounced by Mr. Westlake to be probably correct.[2]

TRINITY CHAPEL AND BECKET'S CROWN.

"And now I shall desire that you would take notice of the Windowes, especially in the Churche's upper part, which both for the glasse and Iron-worke thereof are well worthy of your observation. This part of the Church was highly commended by Malmesbury in his time, amongst other

---

[1] Gostling, p. 327. [2] Westlake, p. 69.

things, for this ornament.   Nihil tale possit in Anglia videri,
etc., saith he.   And I think his words hold true still (1640).
And I beleeve as much may be said of the Iron-worke about
them, apparently various, and offer to our view certaine verses
containing a parallel of the old and new Testament." [1]

The windows are supposed to date from 1220-1240.[2]

Their Origin.

Mr. Westlake says : "There are histories of S. Thomas
very similar to those in many churches of France, and some
fragments of a series remain at Lincoln.   Those at Chartres
and Sens especially abound in such close resemblances of
design and detail, that I am convinced they were designed
and executed by the same hand as the Canterbury work, and
that the windows or the artists were imported into England
from France." [3]

" It would be an easy matter for any package of glass to
have been transplanted from either Sens or Chartres to
England.   Sens is on the river Vanne, which falls into the
Yonne close by ; this falls into the Seine at Fontainebleau." [4]

" At Fordwich (on the Stour) the Prior and Convent of
Canterbury were, at the time of their suppression, possessed
of a marsh here, called Prior's Marsh, containing 20 acres.
Fordwich was a great resort for ships.   The ships were
moored there, and laden and unladen.   In 1285, a com-
position was made between the Prior and Abbot of S.
Augustine's about the customs.   The Prior of Canterbury
had a house upon the shore." [5]

The intercourse between Canterbury and Chartres is
shown by the following extract :—

" In July, 1176, the Dean of Chartres, with the members
of his chapter, came to Canterbury.   Their bishop being

[1] Somner, p. 175.   [2] Westlake, p. 110.
[3] *Ibid.*, vol. i., pp. 107-8.   [4] *Ibid.*, vol. i., p. 127.
                [5] Hasted, vol. iii., p. 604.

THE TOMB IN THE CRYPT.

Plate 10.

dead, they came to beg that Becket's friend and counsellor, John, Archdeacon of Salisbury, might be permitted to occupy the vacant See." [1]

The Stories.

The stories of the miracles are taken from the collections mentioned beneath.

" Within a few years after the death of Archbishop Thomas, two collections of his miracles were produced by monks of his Cathedral Church. The first was by Benedict, afterwards Prior of Canterbury, and eventually Abbot of Peterborough ; the other was by William, and although Benedict appears to have been both earlier in time and more eminent as a member of the monastic community, it would seem that William's narration of the miracles was considered as the more important of the two, on account probably of its greater extent, and also of a kind of official authority which it derived from having been presented by the monks of Christ Church to King Henry II." [2] " It would seem that William held some office in connection with the tomb of S. Thomas, as we find him receiving pilgrims and listening to their stories." [3]   " Benedict, after having been chancellor (or secretary) to Archbishop Richard, became Prior of Christ Church, Canterbury, in 1175." [4]   " Like William, he seems to have held office in connection with the tomb." [5]

The Tomb of Becket in the Crypt.

" The tomb was in the easternmost part of Ernulf's Crypt. The sick were admitted to visit it for the first time on 2nd April, 1171." " For 50 years it continued to be the central object of interest for crowds of Canterbury pilgrims

---

[1] Scott Robertson, p. 36.   [2] Robertson, vol. i., xxvii.
[3] *Ibid.*, vol. i., xxx.   [4] *Ibid.*, vol. ii., p. 19.
[5] *Ibid.*, vol. ii., xxiii.

between 1170 and 1220." [1]   " The monks erected around it strong walls, formed of great stones firmly compacted with mortar, lead and iron.   Two window-like apertures were left in each of the four walls, and through them pilgrims, by inserting their heads, might kiss the sarcophagus.   These apertures are represented in some coloured windows of the choir as being of oval shape.   Over the top of the enclosing walls a huge stone was placed.   It was so arranged that between this top stone and the lid of the sarcophagus a concave structure intervened, affording a hollow space about twelve inches deep.   Into this shallow space some pilgrims managed to creep through one of the windows, expecting to receive greater benefit from close contact with the coffin itself." [2]   " After the fire, as the older Trinity Chapel was swept away in order to make room for the larger and more beautiful work, a temporary wooden chapel was constructed around the tomb until the time should come when the body might be translated to the shrine erected by Walter of Colchester and Elias of Dereham in the completed building of William the Englishman." [3]

" When the saint's blood had been found to possess a miraculous power, there was a fear lest it should be soon exhausted.   This fear suggested the experiment of mixing it with water, and that the minutest drop of the sacred blood gave to the mass of water a share of its own miraculous efficacy." [4]

" At first the water was put in wooden boxes, sometimes with little mirrors.   Afterwards, as they leaked, leaden bottles (ampulle) were used and became the token of the Pilgrims." [5]

The twelve windows in the Trinity Chapel were originally " filled with glass representing the miracles of Becket ".   The Auditor of the Cathedral, William Somner, writes in 1640 :

---

[1] *The Crypt of Canterbury Cathedral*, by Canon Scott Robertson, pp. 32-34.
[2] *Ibid.*, p. 34.   [3] Robertson, vol. ii., xxxviii.
[4] *Ibid.*, vol. ii., xxx.   [5] *Ibid.*, xxxi.

" the legend of whose miracles, were it utterly lost, might easily, I think, be replaced from the windows on each side of the place where the shrine sometime stood, abounding altogether with the story thereof".

Two years later,[1] the great destruction took place, beginning " with the windowe on the east of the high altar, and many window-Images or pictures in glasse were demolished that day ".

In 1660 Somner writes again : " The windowes famous for strength and beauty generally battered and broken, as they lay exposed to the injury of all weathers ".

In 1721 they are spoken of as " so mended and confused as not to afford much speculation ".[2]

In 1772 the windows on the north side are said to have been " preserved by the buildings adjacent from that destruction which those on the south have suffered ". In one window a " pretty regular series of transactions concerning the martyrdom and burial of Becket may be traced ".[3]

Hasted says : " They were designed to represent the passion of S. Thomas with the story of his miracles. Part of the glass on the north side of Becket's Chapel remains yet ; great part has been destroyed, and though the windows in Becket's Crown appear at a little distance entire, yet they have suffered in many places, and have been but very awkwardly mended." [4] For some time the lower parts of the remaining windows, to the height of about three medallions, were plain white quarries.[5] Later, perhaps in 1799, some medallions were removed to the triforium, some to the north and south choir transepts, and two to the south transept in the nave. The late Mr. George Austin re-arranged in part the three Becket windows and the east window, which was " black and broken," filling up the vacancies with new subjects or copies of the old.

---

[1] Aug. 26, 1642.—*Cathedral Newes.*   [2] Dart, p. 32.
[3] Barnby, p. 37.   [4] Hasted, vol. iv., p. 529.
[5] The blank spaces partly represented in Wild's *Perspective Views*, p. 14.

BECKET'S CROWN.

EAST WINDOW.

The subjects represented in the east window are the Crucifixion, the Entombment, the Resurrection, the Ascension

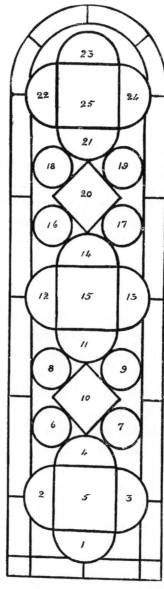

PLAN 10.

and Pentecost, each surrounded by four types. Five of the
medallions are new, but all available old fragments were
introduced. The scrolls at the base are new, and two lengths
of bordering on either side. These were placed when the
whole window, which was " black and broken," was re-leaded
about 1853 by Mr. Caldwell, under the direction of his
master, the late Mr. George Austin. The border much
resembles one at Soissons and also one at Bourges,
" and the panel of the Spies is very much like one at
Chartres ".[1]

    1. The Spies. The heads are both new and also the
pink drapery.
    2. Moses striking the Rock. ⎞ Are all in their original
    3. The Paschal Lamb.   ⎬   state.
    4. The Sacrifice of Isaac. ⎠
    5. The Crucifixion. From a design in Mr. Austin's
possession.
    10. The Entombment is unrestored.
    6. Joseph in the Well. The head of Joseph and parts
of the drapery are new.
    7. Daniel in Babylon.   ⎞
    8. Samson and Delilah. ⎬ Are unrestored.
    9. Jonah cast into the Sea.⎠
    15. The centre subject—The Resurrection—is new, also
the subjects on either side.
    12. Noah receiving the Dove is new ; had "all
gone".
    13. The Escape of the Spies is new.
    11. The Burning Bush and Moses is old.
    14. The Landing of Jonah is old. But his drapery is
new, and the whale received a new head.
    20. The centre subject—The Ascension. Some of the
heads are new.

[1] Westlake.

16. The Ark of the Mercy-seat. ⎫
17. The Burial of Moses.   ⎪
18. The Ascension of Elijah.   ⎪
19. The Sundial of Ahaz.   ⎬   Are all unrestored.
25. Pentecost.   ⎪
21. The Giving of the Law.   ⎪
22. The Ordination of Deacons.   ⎭
23. Our Lord in Majesty is new.
24. The First Council is unrestored.

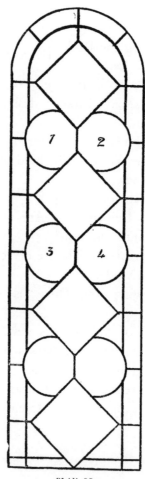

PLAN II.

Third Window. Trinity Chapel, North Side.

Four medallions. Eight of the upper roundels and part
of the border are original. The remainder is the work of
Mr. Caldwell, from old fragments, 1894.

1 and 2. Represent pilgrims on their way to the shrine.
There are many stories of shipwrecked mariners and of
others, who, on their way to Compostella, were repulsed by
furious winds and brought back to Sandwich harbour, when
the Crosses destined for S. James were presented to the shrine
of the " liberator," S. Thomas.[1]

3. A king resting on a bed may possibly represent
Henry II. relating his vision to Benedict, who is standing
by holding a scroll with an inscription.[2] " In consequence
of his vision, and reflecting on the accidents and dangers
which happen to mortals, with promises unfulfilled, he grants
to the Church the liberties he had promised." [3] The head
of the king is of a later date.

4. Represents a cure.

Fourth Window.

The ground is diapered. Three lengths on either of the
side borders are new.

1. An offering at the tomb.

2. The saint with a nimbus feeling the pulse of a man in
bed. Inscription—Qua dolet, hac planat ; dolet his tribus,
et tria sanat. (Where it pains, there he smooths. It pains
in these three places, and he heals the three.)

3. A woman is being dragged by two others towards a
woman under a portico. Partly new.

4. A woman sitting down with her feet in a bowl. A

---

[1] Bened. II., p. 112.   [2] Will. I., p. 493.
[3] A clause was inserted in one of the treaties between Louis VII. and
Henry II. allowing one of Louis' best artists in glass to come to England.
Westlake, vol. i., p. 39.

figure kneels before her with a towel.   Three other figures, one holding a bowl and another a bottle for the water.

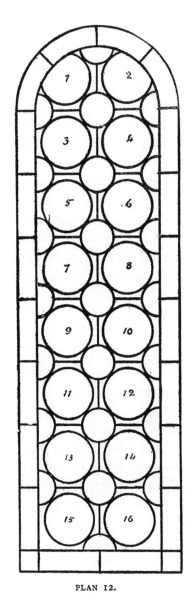

PLAN 12.

5, 6, 7, 8. Are all new copies of the story of William of Kellett.

9. A figure, supported by another, is kneeling with clasped hands before a priest at the altar.

10. The same figure kneeling at the altar. He has taken off his green drapery. The right leg is diseased, the other has a red stocking and yellow shoe. A priest addresses him. Before them is a shoe. The inscription is— est baculus, vestis, pero cunctis ibi testis. (The crutch, coat, boot is a witness there to all men.) The story probably relates to Robert of Cricklade, Prior of S. Frideswide. He was walking " beside the Adriatic Sea when the surf of the sea gave him a swelling on the foot with a very bad in- flammation, so that he could not put on or draw off his boot without great pain ".[1] He was cured by anointing his foot with the holy water (see Story III.). This story was one which made its way to Iceland.[2]

11. A lady in a chair in great exhaustion. A friend or nurse sitting by her and a priest addresses her. His head, the candlesticks and the pink drapery new.

12. The lady kneels and offers a coil.[3] A priest hastens to meet her.

14. A madman, whose hands are bound with cords, is made to kneel at the tomb. Two men are preparing to beat him. Amens accedit is the inscription.

13. He is quietly kneeling. Sanus recedit is the in- scription. (He comes a madman, but goes away sane.) One of the keepers lifts up his hand in astonishment. The cords and whips lie on the ground no longer needed.

15. Is copied in II.—7. A woman going to drink the holy water. A man standing by explains the case to the priest.

16. The priest is stirring up the draught for a woman

---

[1] Bened. II., p. 97.   [2] Margesson, p. 93.

[3] " It was usual to measure with a thread the body or the affected member of sufferers, and to vow a model, a silver thread, or most fre- quently a wax candle of the like dimensions, to be offered at the tomb." Canon Robertson, ii., xxix.

who is being helped forward by another.   She has presented
a coil.

FIFTH WINDOW.

Six lengths of the border and parts of the lowest scrolling
are new, and quarter circles.

1. The saint appears to Benedict, who is on a couch
beneath.   He is represented emerging from the Shrine.[1]
" It was covered with plates of gold, damasked and embossed
with wires of gold, garnished with broches, images, angels,
chaines, pretious stones and great orient pearls." [2]

2. A man seated on a chair with diseased leg.   One
attendant is washing the leg.   Another brings a bowl,
another a towel.   Detumet in voto lavacro (gravitas) prece,
sanguine, poto.   (In making the vow, the severe swelling is
reduced by prayer and the blood and the draught.)

3. A woman with bare leg about to kneel at the tomb.
Some of the figures are new.   The inscription imperfect, but
conjectured to be—Magnificat sanctum, satiat medicamine
planctum.   (She magnifies the saint, she satisfies the lamentation with medicine.)

4. A man half dressed is sitting in a chair, and bends
forwards to receive some clothes another man is bringing.
Perhaps Godwin of Boxgrove, who distributed all his clothes
that he might be an example of voluntary poverty.[3]

5. The story of a blind lady and her blind attendant
feeling their way to the tomb.

6. The bandages are removed, the staff left behind, and
they are represented turning round to take one more look
as they return.

7, 8, 9. Are all new, being copies of 15, 16, 12 in I.

10, 11, 12. Is the story of two lame damsels, who from
their very cradles had supported themselves on crutches

---

[1] Bened., p. 27.   [2] Stow, quoted by Somner, p. 247.
[3] Will. I., p. 339.

rather than on their feet. They are represented going to
the shrine. While they were both imploring the martyr to

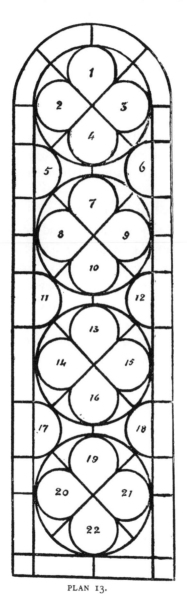

PLAN 13.

heal them, a sleep fell upon the elder. The saint promised
her health and granted it. She is represented giving thanks.

The younger blamed the saint, and cried out, " Hast thou
but one blessing ? " etc., and as she wept the holy father came
to her as she slept, (12) and restored her to health.[1] (The
saint is new.).

The Third Circle

Contains the story of Eilward and Fulk, who quarrelled
over a debt.   Eilward breaks into Fulk's house and is seized
by him and taken before a magistrate.[2]

13. He is riding out of the city.

14. He is brought before two men, who hold him fast
before the judge.

15. His eye is being put out.

17. The saint touches the eye and heals him.

16. He is pointing with one hand to the restored eye,
and with the other giving money to a group of beggars, one
of whom, with legs turned in, supports himself on a board
with irons, as is sometimes seen now.   On the other side,
one man has a purse or wallet and passes the money on to
Eilward.   Dat ille stipes pauperibus.   Perhaps—Sanatus dat
mille stipes pauperibus ille.   (Healed, he gives a thousand
alms to the poor.)

18. Is new.   He is giving thanks.

The Fourth Circle

Contains the story of the physician of Perigord, who was
cured of dropsy by drinking the holy water.[3]

19. He is sitting up in bed, and the priest is bringing it.
Desperant medici, pater (eretes), et morientes amici.   (The
doctors, father and friends of the dying man are hopeless.)

20. The physician receiving the last Sacraments.   Part
of the figures are new ; the one behind.   Spes desperanti
superest in sanguine sancti.   (To the hopeless there remains

---

[1] Bened. II., p. 170.   [2] *Ibid.*, p. 173.   [3] Will. I., p. 261.

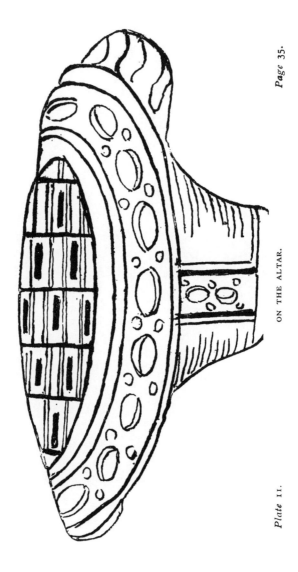

Plate 11.

ON THE ALTAR.

Page 35.

hope in the blood of the saint.)   What is conjectured to be a wafer box is on the altar.

21. He is dying.

22. Is new.   He is giving thanks.   Est baculus vestis pero cre sibi testis pero.

Sixth Window.

The border of this is identical with that of S. Eustace at Sens.   Three lengths of border on each side are new.

1. A man in green tunic and yellow cloak is helping a blind woman.

2. He leads her with difficulty to the tomb, where the priest hastens to give her something.

3. She is restored and talking to the man who led her. The inscription over 1 is—Pastor alendorum curam puer egit equorum.   (The shepherd boy has taken care of the horses to be fed.)   Evidently it might belong to the story beneath.

4. Represents a man driving four horses.   The trees meet on either side of the road.

5. He is sleeping under a tree, and the horses are left to themselves.   Over is—Sanctus sopitur lepras $\begin{cases} \text{vulnusque} \\ \text{ulcuçque} \end{cases}$ operitur.   (Misplaced.)   (The saint soothes the leprosy and covers over the $\begin{cases} \text{wound.} \\ \text{ulcer.} \end{cases}$)

5. Perhaps the story of an Irish soldier, Walter, who turned his horses loose in the enclosure of a Chapel dedicated to the saint at Dublin without any one to look after them. The horses were stolen, " and he very nearly accused the martyr Thomas, as he had trusted to him, but believing more was to be done by invocations than accusations, he took refuge in prayer," and the robber, who was carrying off the horses, lost his way and found himself back in the place

in the morning where he had committed the robbery, and so he set the horses free and fled.[1]

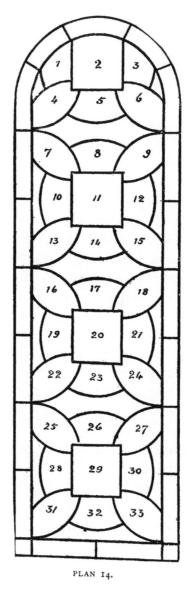

PLAN 14.

6. A man in bed holding out his hands for some clothes which a woman is bringing to him on a tray. The woman's

[1] Will. I., p. 545.

mouth is covered.   Omnibus abjectus vix sic a matre re-
fectus.   (Cast out by all men, he is thus hardly revived by
his mother.)

7. A man and woman standing at the tomb, before which
a young man is kneeling.

8. Two men address a knight and lady.

9. A young man making an offering at the tomb.

10, 11, 12. Are new, and copies from the story beneath
of the knight Jordan.   In 12 the woman is original.

13, 14, 15. Is the story of a boy at Rochester, named
Robert, who had been drowned in the Medway.   The boys,
who have been pelting frogs in the sedges, are shouting that
Robert has slipped in the river.   He is disappearing in the
water beside three large green frogs.[1]

2. The boys run and tell the mother, who exclaims :
"Gracious Thomas, martyr of God, restore to me my son !"

3. He had fallen in at the ninth hour and at that of
vespers.   He was pulled out by a man with an iron hook.
(He offers a silver thread.[2])   The mother is holding out her
hands to receive the body of her child ; the father behind.

16, 17, 18. Are new.   16 is a copy of 7.   17 is the
story of Richard the Smith, cured of blindness.   18. His
offering.

19. A maniac woman struggling between two men who
are about to beat her with sticks.   Perhaps—Alternant
mentem, gestum quoque vincla furentein.   (Chains make
her ⎰
his ⎱ mind, and ⎰her⎱ mad bearing too, come and go.)
             ⎱his⎰

20. The figure is falling fainting to the ground.   One
of the attendants is still striking her, the other addressing
the priest, who is reading.   Stat modo jucunda (quae) lapsa
jacet moribunda.

21. She is bowing before the priest at the altar, who
is receiving a large candle apparently offered by her.   Two

<hr>

[1] Bened. II., p. 226.   [2] *Ibid.*, p. 227.

men with long robes stand by.   Perhaps the story " of a little woman named Matilda possessed by a devil, and we shrunk from her as she showed her madness before our very eyes ".[1]

22, 23, 24. Are copies from the story of the physician of Périgord in the fifth window.

The next nine compartments are the history of the household of a distinguished knight Jordan.[2]

31. The nurse dies.   The body, covered by a large yellow pall, is borne on a bier carried by four men.   A second priest is bearing a huge lighted taper.   The inscription is—Nutricis funus reliquis sui flagra minatur. Then the son dies, a boy of ten.

32. He is stretched on a bier, the priest at the head anoints the body with holy water, and on the forehead of the child is the Viaticum or sacred wafer.   The mother absorbed in deep grief, and the father wringing his hands. Perculitur puer moritur planetus geminatur.   There arrived that day twenty pilgrims from whom the father borrowed some diluted water.

· 33. The mother stands at the head of the bier.   The father pours between the clenched lips the wonder-working blood and water.   The pilgrims reverently gazing.   Vox patris, vis martiris ut restituatur.   A small spot of red showed itself on the left cheek of the boy.   He opened one eye and said : " Why are you weeping, father ?   Why are you crying, Lady ?   The blessed martyr Thomas has restored me to you."

25. The father puts into his son's hands four pieces of silver to be an offering to the martyr before Mid Lent.

26. The son is upon a couch fast recovering, feeding himself with a spoon and bason.   But the vow is forgotten.

27. A leper three miles off is aroused from slumber by a voice calling him by name : " Guirp, why sleepest thou ? "

[1] Bened. II., p. 208.
[2] Dean Stanley ; Will. I., p. 160 ; Bened. II., p. 229.

and tells him he must go and warn the knight Jordan of the evils that would befall him unless he instantly performed the vow.

28. The leper is in bed, conveying to the parents the warning. They fix the last week in Lent for the performance of the vow. But a visit of the Lord Warden puts it out of their heads. The boy dies and twenty of the household fell sick. Credutis accedis vot, fert nec obedit.

29. At the head and feet of the corpse are the figures, probably professional mourners. Unseen is the figure of S. Thomas. He bears in his hand a sword. Vindicte moles Domus egra et mortua proles. (Weight of punishment— household sick and offspring dead.)

30. The accomplishment of the vow. The father is offering a large bowl full of gold and silver pieces. Near him is the mother holding by the hand the boy, now quite well.

TRINITY CHAPEL (SOUTH SIDE).

First Window, East.

Possibly the six medallions of the Kellett series now in the south triforium, and the Forester in the north, were originally in this window. The eight half circles appear to belong to the fifth window, south side, Trinity Chapel, and were placed here to fill up the vacancies after the great destruction. In 1893, by order of the late Dean Payne Smith, the window was completed by Mr. Caldwell, who added eight medallions from fragments of old glass.

1 and 2. In their original position.

3 and 4. By Mr. Caldwell.

5. In two parts. A boat, in which is a figure with a pole. The other half contains fragments of a river scene.

6, 7, and 8. Remains of offerings after cures.

9, 10, 11, 12, 13, 14. By Mr. Caldwell.

15. A bier with yellow handles, covered by a pall. Priests officiating. One with asperge and stoup.

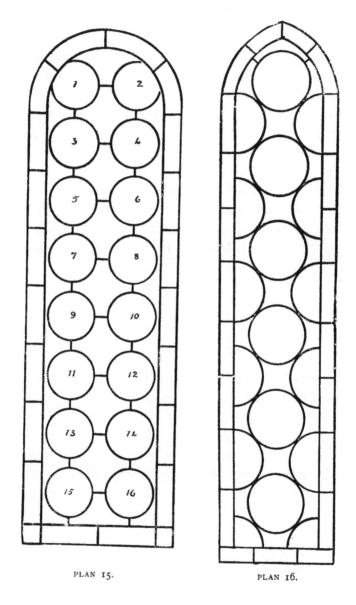

PLAN 15.   PLAN 16.

16. In two parts. To the right a father embracing his little boy. The mother lifting up her hands in wonder.

THE FEVER.

Plate 12.   *Page* 41

THE OFFERING.

Plate 13.   Page 41.

THE FALL OF THE WALL.

Plate 14.

THE MOTHER FAINTS.

Plate 15.   *Page* 41.

Perhaps the story of the Welsh soldier's son Ranulf.[1] To the left a man is bending forward offering a coil. The figures of the priests imperfect.

In addition to the medallions, Mr. Caldwell added eight pieces of bordering, three on each side and two at the bottom, also the spandrels at the bottom.

THE SIXTH WINDOW, SOUTH SIDE.

Twelve of these medallions were placed (probably in the beginning of this century) in windows in the north and south choir transepts, which were cut to receive them. In 1897, by order of the Dean and Chapter, they were restored to their original position in the Trinity Chapel, where four medallions and some scrolling had remained. Six medallions were made by Mr. Caldwell, partly from fragments of old glass, to fill up the vacant spaces. He also completed the border, of which only a small portion remained, and which had been transferred to the transept windows to lengthen them. The original borders of the transept windows still remain there.

1. Godfrey of Winchester has a fever, but is cured by the holy water. Thomae virtute vis febris cedit acutae. (The force of severe fever is overcome by the power of S. Thomas.)[2]

2. His offering. Auxilium pietas fert quod sibi non sinit aetas. (Piety brings the help which age does not allow to itself.)

3. While he is asleep in the cradle the wall of the house falls. Ecce repentina premitur puer ipse ruina. (Lo, the boy himself is overwhelmed by the sudden downfall.)

4. New. The mother prays : " O Saint Thomas, preserve my boy ".

6. The mother shrieks and faints.

---

[1] Will. I., p. 209.   [2] *Ibid.*, p. 206.

5. Two old servants passing by dig away the ruins, and lift up the boy unhurt.

PLAN 18.

PLAN 19.

PLAN 17.

7. New. A certain woman tells the grandmother he must be taken to the saint's tomb, as he is ill again.

THE DELIVERANCE.

Plate 16.   Page 42.

THE OFFERING AT THE TOMB.

Plate 17.

Page 43.

SVPPLEX IMPLO   UI9H PEONNSH OONII

A CRIPPLE AT THE TOMB.

Plate 18.   *Page* 43.

A LEPER PRIEST.

Plate 19.

Page 43.

THE FALL OF EARTH ON WILLIAM OF GLOUCESTER.

Plate 20.   *Page* 43.

TWO MEN BRING THE NEWS THAT HE IS DEAD.

Plate 21.   *Page* 43.

A DISMAL GROAN IS HEARD.

THE GOOD NEWS IS TOLD.

Plate 23.   *Page* 43.

MEN ARRIVE WITH COUNTRY TOOLS.

Plate 24.

Page 43.

WILLIAM IS BROUGHT OUT.

Plate 25.   *Page* 43.

A LADY OFFERING A COIL.

Plate 26.　　　　　　　　　　　　　　　　　*Page* 43.

A LADY KNEELING AT AN ALTAR.

Plate 27.   Page 43.

8. He is brought there. Ventri intestinam monumentum dat medecinam. (The tomb gives internal healing to the stomach.)

9. A cripple coming to the tomb. Possibly Eilwin of Berkhampstead.[1]

10. He is cured.

11. New. A leper priest of Reading meets some pilgrims returning from Canterbury.[2]

12. They give him some of the holy water.

13. The story of William of Gloucester, who, in making an aqueduct, was buried beneath a fall of earth at Churchdown.

13. The earth falls on William.

14. Two men bring the news that he is dead.

15. New. A woman tells her son she knows he is not dead, but drinking milk. The son meets the watchman of the fields.

16. They hear a dismal groan.

17. New. Roger the priest arrives and sends messengers with the news to Gloucester.

18. The women are told. Miratur multum populus spirare sepultum. (The crowd greatly wonder that the buried man is breathing.)

19. All holy and humble men of heart come with spades and country tools.

20. He is brought back to the world. Thomam quem dicit ereptorem benedicit. (He blesses Thomas, whom he calls his deliverer.)

21. A lady offering a coil at a small altar.

22. A lady kneeling at another altar.

---

[1] Bened. II., p. 124. [2] Will. I., p. 416.

WINDOW IN SOUTH TRANSEPT OF NAVE.

Between 1382 and 1400 "the nave and western transepts completed by Prior Chillenden, assisted by Archbishops
Courtney and Arundel ".[1]

"This window has been lately rebuilt at the cost of
£1000."

"In 1799 this window was selected and arranged with
much care and industry by Mr. John Simmonds, one of the

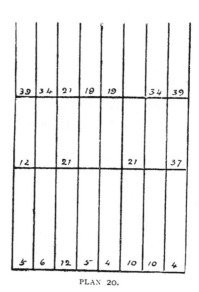

PLAN 20.

vesturers of this Church, to whom the arrangement was
committed by the Dean (Powys) and Chapter."[2]

"The large perpendicular window in the S. Transept of
the Nave is filled with medallions and pieces of border taken
from the Clerestory of the Choir Transepts, with exception
of some small fragments of the canopies originally surmount-

---

[1] Conspectus. "In the fourteenth century there was a centre (for glass)
in Kent, possibly at Canterbury or Dover. There were doubtless many large
and important ateliers at that time, and it is fairly evident that not only
Englishmen, but artists of other countries, were employed in them. It
seems to have been quite a conservative atelier." Westlake, vol. ii., p. 41.

[2] Hasted, p. 529, ed. 1799, note.

ing the figures which once filled it." [1]   The mark * shows which were reglazed by Mr. Caldwell between 1859 to the present time, 1897.   The numbers correspond with those in the plan of the choir.

UPPER TIER, BEGINNING FROM THE LEFT.

39 [(1)] *Joanna.   The green drapery is new and part of the white.   Beneath—fifteenth century angel with yellow suns.   Probably this and similar ones are from quatrefoils in the windows of the nave.

34 [(2)] Sher.   Beneath—Dean and Chapter coat of arms. Archbishop's coat of arms above.

21 [(3)] *Josias.   The head is new.   Beneath—fifteenth century angel with suns.

19 [(4)] *David.

19 [(5)] Nathan.   New head.   Arms of Archbishop above.

[(6)] Unidentified.   New head.   Beneath—fifteenth century angel.

34 [(7)] Jose.

39 [(8)] Juda.   Beneath—feathered angel with suns.

MIDDLE TIER.

12 [(1)] Abram.

[(2)] Unidentified.   Royal shield above.

21 [(3)] Ezechias.   Archbishop's coat of arms beneath.

[(4)] Archbishop Abbott's coat of arms above, and miracles, probably from window in the Trinity Chapel, and the ruby chequer and blue rosettes from the clerestory.

[(5)] Above—coat of arms of Kingsley.

21 [(6)] Royal shield above.   Josias.   Archbishop's coat of arms beneath.

[(7)] Above—three beavers.   Unidentified.   New head.

[(8)] Royal shield above.   Zerobabel. [2]

---

[1] Felix Summerley, p. 108, 1860.
[2] 37 in Gostling; 38 in Austin's plan.

Lowest Tier.

Royal shields above all, but incorrectly given, with the exception of Nos. 4 and 5.

5 [(1).] Lamech.

6 [(2).] Noe.

12 [(3).] Thare.

5 [(4).] Methusaleh.

4 [(5).] Jareth or Jared.

10 [(6).] Phalec.

10 [(7).] *Ragan.   New head, hands and part of drapery.

4 [(8).] Enoch.

The designs beneath were reglazed by Mr. Caldwell, and parts of some of the medallions were restored by him.   The coats of arms not mentioned are either modern additions or old fragments incorrectly put together.

THE WEST WINDOW OF THE NAVE.

" 1382 to 1400.   The stained glass in the great west window of the Nave is of this period, but fragments of earlier glass have been inserted." [1]

Under the point of the arch are the arms of Richard II. impaling those of his patron saint, Edward the Confessor. The next range consists of six small figures between the arms of the two wives of Richard II., Anne of Bohemia to the north and Isabella of France to the south.   The next two ranges were filled with Saints and the Apostles.[2]   Now they are replaced by Saints and Bishops said to have been brought, about 1799, from the west window in the Chapter House. The Seven Kings are in the next range.   Beginning from the right, the order is—Canute, Edward the Confessor holding a book, Harold, William I. with sceptre, William II., Henry I., Stephen.[3]   Below are more figures from the Chapter House, and the medallions removed about 1799 from the clerestory. The numbers correspond with the MS. catalogue of Mr.

[1] Conspectus.   [2] Gostling, p. 343.
[3] *Chronological History of Canterbury Cathedral*, by G. Smith, p. 381.

George Austin. The coats of arms are composed of old fragments and modern pieces put together at the time when the window was refilled. The row at the bottom are royal shields.[1]

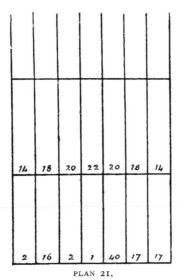

PLAN 21.

To the Left, Upper Tier.

14 [1]. Juda.

18 [2]. Obeth.

20 [3]. Roboas.   Reglazed by Mr. Caldwell.

22 [4]. Jeconias.

20 [5]. Perhaps Abias.   Not identified.

18 [6]. Jesse.

14 [7]. Phares.

Lower Tier.

2 [1]. Enos.

16 [2]. Naason.

2 [3]. Seth.

1 [4]. Adam.   ⎫

40 [5]. Semei or Joseph. ⎬ Also reglazed by Mr. Caldwell.

                                      ⎭

17 [6]. Salmon.

17 [7]. Boaz.

[1] Felix Summerley, p. 107.

WINDOW IN THE NORTH TRANSEPT OF NAVE.

1470-1480. "Stained glass in the great north window of west transept."[1]

"This goodly and glorious window, a piece of its kinde beyond compare," was given by Edward IV. in memory of the marriage of Edward I. and Marguerite of France.[2]

Beneath the point of the arch are two shields, one of France and England, quarterly, the other of Canterbury impaling the arms of Bourchier.

The next three ranges represent—1. Prophets; 2. Apostles; 3. Bishops.[3]

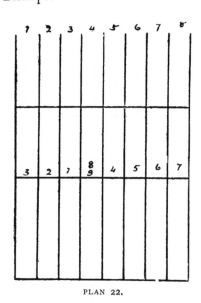

PLAN 22.

Beneath are angels bearing shields.

1. The arms of Dean and Chapter.

2. The arms of Guldeford and Halden.

3. Canterbury, impaling a chevron between three crows. "As this was the bearing of Becket, here was probably his effigies" (reversed).

[1] Conspectus. Scott-Robertson.   [2] Somner, p. 166.
[3] Gostling, p. 332.

4. The monkish device of the Trinity, under which we may suppose was the representation of God the Father and of Christ, besides a large Crucifix and the picture of the Holy Ghost in the form of a Dove mentioned by Culmer.

5. The arms of Edward the Confessor.

6. The framework of a well, being the arms of Cecilia, daughter of Edward I., who married Viscount Wells.

7. The arms of an Archbishop, made by Mr. Caldwell. Beneath are seven angels bearing shields.

1. Royal arms with argent label for Prince of Wales.[1]

2. Royal arms.   Edward IV.

3. Royal arms, a label of three points, argent, the dexter point charged with a canton, gules.   Duke of York.

4. Gules, three crowns in pale, or, Ethelred.

5. Fragments of the arms of Castile and Leon.

6. Royal arms, impaling those of Elizabeth Woodville.

7. The arms of Mortimer and Burgh.

In the next range—1. Is modern ; 2. An Archbishop's ; 3. Royal shield (incorrect) ; 4. Modern ; 5. Dean and Chapter ; 6, 7. Illegible.

In the range below is the family of King Edward IV.

In the middle compartment was the large Crucifix before which the royal family were kneeling.   The figures have all new heads, and much of the drapery and other parts have been restored by Mr. Caldwell, under the direction of the late Mr. Harry Austin, the surveyor of the Cathedral. Parts of the original figures are in the hall at the Deanery, having been removed there in 1879.

1. To the left is the effigy of Edward IV.   The curtain at the back of the King has the rose in sun, " the device he took in memory of the battle of Mortimer's Cross, where there were seen three suns immediately conjoining in one ". Underneath—Edwardus dei gracia Rex Anglia et Francia et dominus hiberniae.[2]

[1] Willement.   [2] Gostling, p. 336.

2. The Prince of Wales has his half curtain covered with single feathers in stripes.

3. To the left, the Duke of York has his curtain covered with a falcon in fetlock, or, on a background, azure.

4. The Queen has sprigs of broom vert, in a cloud gules and placed on an azure ground.

5, 6, 7. To the right of the Queen are three Princesses kneeling.

8, 9. In the centre, above the coat of arms of Henry VII., are two figures in niches—a king in armour with a sword, Mauritius underneath, and a female figure with long hair, helmet and sword.

In the next range " the seven glorious appearances of the Virgin Marie were pictured beneath ".

The coats of arms are—1. Becket ; 2. Royal arms ; 3. The arms of an Archbishop ; 4. Royal arms ; 5. The arms of the Scotts of Scot's Hall, three Catherine wheels ; 6. Royal arms ; 7. Modern.

In the centre of the third and fifth lights are the arms of two Archbishops.

A description of this window is given by Richard Culmer in 1644, two years after he had destroyed it. It is taken from the *Cathedrall Newes from Canterbury*.[1]

" The work of destruction in the Cathedral had begun at the east end, and had proceeded as far as the screen between the choir and the nave, when it was interrupted by a Prebend's wife, who pleaded for the Images and jeered the Commissioners viragiously. She shreekt out and ran to her husband, who, after she was gone, came in and asked for their authoritie to doe these things. After he had disputed a while, the grand Priest complained for want of breath, saying he was ready to faint, and desired to be let out. And indeed he looked very ill. Then the work of Reformation went on, and the Commissioners fell presently to work on the great idolatrous window. In that window was now the picture of God the Father, and of Christ, besides a large

Crucifix and the pictures of the Holy Ghost in the form of a Dove and of the twelve Apostles. And in that window were seen seven large pictures of the Virgin Marie, in seven several glorious appearances as of the Angells lifting her into Heaven, and the Sun, Moon, and Stars under her feet, and every picture had an inscription under it, beginning with gaude Maria—as gaude Maria, sponsa dei, that is, rejoice Mary, Spouse of God. There were in this window many other pictures of Popish Saints, as of S. George, etc. But their prime Cathedrall saint, Arch Bishop Thomas Becket, was most rarely pictured in that window, in full proportion, with cope, Rochet, miter, Crosier and all his Pontificalibus. And in the foot of that window was a tittle, intimating that window to be dedicated to the Virgin Mary. While judgment was executing on the Idols in that window, the Cathedralists cryed out again for their great Diana, hold your hands, holt, holt, heers, Sirs, etc. A minister being then on the top of the citie ladder, near 60 steps high, with a whole pike in his hand, ratling down proud Becket's glassy bones, others then present would not adventer so high, to him it was said, 'tis a shame for a Minister to be seen there. The Minister replyed, Sir, I count it no shame, but an honour, my Master whipt the living buyers and sellers out of the Temple, these are dead Idylls, which defile the worship of God here, being the fruits and occasions of idolatry. Some wisht he might break his neck, others said, it should cost blood. But he finished the worke and came downe well, and was in very good health when this was written."

THE DEAN'S CHAPEL AND S. MICHAEL'S.

Formerly called the Lady Chapel or S. Mary's. Built by Prior Goldstone, *circa* 1449-1468.[1]

The east window has five lights. The upper part has

---

[1] Canon Scott-Robertson; Conspectus.

roundels impanelling a golden falcon volant and knots, the badge of the Bourchier family. (Archdeacon Bourchier, who died in 1495, is buried here.) In the lower part, the double knot and a stem of oak leaved and fructed for Woodstock. The Archbishop Bourchier's mother was daughter of Thomas Woodstock, Duke of Gloucester. A border of oak leaves surrounds the window. At the base of the five lights there are five coats of arms, arranged chevron-wise, the highest being in the centre.[1]

THE WARRIOR'S CHAPEL, OR THE SOMERSET OR S. MICHAEL'S CHAPEL.

The east window formerly had the devices of Margaret Holland, who is buried in the Chapel.

THEOLOGICAL WINDOWS.

From a MS. in the library of Corpus Christi College at Oxford. Folio 185.

Fenestrae in superiori parte ecclesiae Christi Cant. incipientes a parte septentrionali.

Fenestra Prima.

1. Moses cum Rubo. In medio. Angelus cum Maria. Rubus non consumitur, tua nec comburitur in carne virginitas.

2. Gedeon cum vellere et conca. Vellus coelestirore maduit, dum puellae venter intumuit.

3. Misericordia et veritas. In medio Maria et Elizabeth.

> Plaude puer puero, virgo vetulae, quia vero
> Obviat hic pietas : veteri dat lex nova metas.

[1] G. Smith.

4. Justitia et Pax.
>Applaudit Regi previsor gratia legi.
>Oscula Justitiae dat pax ; cognata Mariae.

5. Nabugodonosor et lapis cum statua. Puer in praesepio.
>Ut Regi visus lapis est de monte recisus.
>Sic gravis absque viro virgo parit ordine miro.

6. In medio Maria.

7. Moses cum virga. In medio. Angelus et Pastores.
>Ut contra morem dedit arida virgula florem
>Sic virgo puerum, verso parit ordine rerum.

8. David. Gaudebunt campi et omnia quae in eis sunt.

9. Abacuc. Operuit coelos gloria ejus, etc.

Fenestra Secunda.

1. In medio tres Reges equitantes. Balaam. Orietur stella ex Jacob, et exurget homo de Israel. Isaia et Jeremia, Ambulabunt gentes in lumine tuo, etc.

2. In medio. Herodes et Magi. Christus et Gentes.
>Qui sequuntar me non ambulabunt in tenebris.
>Stella Magos duxit, et eos ab Herode reduxit
>Sic Sathanam gentes fugiunt, te Christe sequentes.[1]

3. Pharaoh et Moses, cum populo exiens ab Egipto.
>Exit ab erumna populus ducente columna.
>Stella Magos duxit. Lux Christus utrisque reluxit.

4. In medio. Maria cum puero. Magi et Pastores. Joseph et fratees sui cum Egiptiis.
>Ad te longinquos Joseph trahis at que propinquos.
>Sic Deus in cunis Judaeos gentibus unis.

5. Rex Solomon et Regina Saba.
>Hiis donis donat Regina domum Solomonis.
>Sic Reges Domino dant munera tres, tria, trino.

---

[1] This inscription is now on the adjoining medallion—The Conversion of the Heathen.

6. Admoniti sunt Magi ne Herodem adeant : Propheta et Rex Jeroboam immolans.

> Ut via mutetur redeundo Propheta monetur
> Sic tres egerunt qui Christo dona tulerunt.

7. Subversio Sodomae et Loth fugiens.

> Ut Loth salvetur ne respiciat prohibetur.
> Sic vitant revehi per Herodis regna Sabei.

8. Oblatio pueri in templo, et Simeon. Melchisedech offerens panem et vinum pro Abraham.

> Sacrum quod cernis sacris fuit umbra modernis.
> Umbra fugit. Quare ? quia Christus sistitur arae.

9. Oblatio Samuel.

> Natura geminum triplex oblatio trinum
> Significat Dominum Samuel puer, amphora vinum.

10. Fuga Domini in Egiptum. Fuga David et Doeg.

> Hunc Saul infestat : Saul Herodis typus extat.
> Iste typus Christi, cujus fuga consonat isti.

11. Elias Jesabel et Achab.

> Ut trucis insidias Jesabel declinat Elias.
> Sic Deus Herodem, terrore remotus eodem.

12. Occisio Innocentum. Occisio sacerdotum Domini sub Saul.

> Non cecidit David, pro quo Saul hos jugulavit.
> Sic non est caesus cum caesis transfuga Jesus.

13. Occisio Tribus Benjamin in Gabaon.

> Ecce Rachel nati fratrum gladiis jugulati
> His sunt signati pueri sub Herode necati.

Fenestra Tertia.

1. Jesus sedes in medio Doctorum. Moses et Jethro cum populo.

> Sic Moses audit Jethro vir sanctus obaudit
> Gentiles verbis humiles sunt forma superbis.

2. Daniel in medio seniorum.

> Mirantur pueri seniores voce doceri
> Sic responsa Dei sensum stupent Pharisei.

3. Baptizatur Dominus. Noah in archa.
   Fluxa cuncta vago submergens prima vorago
   Omnia purgavit : Baptisma significavit.
4. Submersio Pharaonis et transitus populi.
   Unda maris rubri spatio divisa salubri
   Quae mentem mundam facit à vitio notat undam.
5. Temptatio gulae et vana gloriae.   Eva capiens
fructum.
   Qui temptat Jesum movet Evam mortis adesum
   Eva gulae cedit, sed non ita Jesus obedit.
6. Eva comedit.
   Victores hic Sathana : movet Evam gloria vana
   Sed quo vicisti te vicit gratia Christi.
7. Tentatio cupiditatis. Adam et Eva comedunt. David
et Goliah.
   Quo Sathan hos subicit Sathanam sapientia vicit
   Ut Goliam David, Sathanam Christus superavit.

FENESTRA QUARTA.

1. Vocatio Nathanael jacentis sub ficu. Adam et Eva
cum foliis.   Populus sub lege.
   Vidit in hiis Christus sub ficu Nathanaelem.
   Lex tegit hanc plebem, quasi ficus Nathanaelem.
2. Christus mutavit aquam in vinum. Sex hydriae. Sex
aetates mundi.   Sex aetates hominum.
   Hydria metretas capiens est quaelibet aetas,
   Primum signorum Deus hic prodendo suorum.
   Lympha dat historiam, vinum notat allegoriam.
   In vinum morum convertit aquam vitiorum.
3. Piscatore Apostolorum.   S. Petrus cum eccles. de
Iud.   Palus cum ecclesia de gentibus.
   Verbum rete ratis Petri domus haec pietatis.
   Pisces Judaei, qui rete ferant Pharisei
   Illa secundaratis, domus haec est plena beatis
   Retia scismaticus, et quivis scindit iniquus.

4. In medio Jesus legit in Synagoga. Esdras legit legem populo. S^tus. Gregor ordinans lectores.

> Quod promulgavit Moses, legem reparavit
> Esdras amissam : Christus renovavit omissam.
> Quod Christus legit, quasi pro lectoribus egit.
> Exemplo cujus sacer est gradus ordinis hujus.

5. Sermo Domini in monte. Doctores Ecclesiae. Moses suscipit legem.

> Hii montem scandunt Scripturae dum sacra pandunt.
> Christus sublimis docet hos sed vulgus in imis
> Ex hinc inde datur in monte quod inde notatur.
> Christum novisse debemus utramque dedisse.

6. Christus descendens de monte mundat leprosum. Paulus baptizat populum. Heliseus. Naaman et Jordanis.

> Carne Deus tectus quasi vallis ad ima provectus
> Mundat leprosum genus humanum vitiosum.
> Que lavat ecce Deus que mundat et hic Heliseus.
> Est genus humanum Christi baptismate sanum.

FENESTRA QUINTA.

1. Jesus ejicit Demonium. Angelus ligavit Demonium.

> Imperat immundis Deus hic equis furibundis
> Hiis virtus Christi dominatur ut Angelus isti.

2. Maria unxit pedes Chr. Drusiana vestit et pascit egenos.

> Curam languenti, victum qui praebet egenti
> Seque reum plangit, Christi vestigia tangit.
> Illa quod ungendo facit haec sua distribuendo
> Dum quod de pleno superest largitur egeno.

3. Marta et Maria cum Jesu. Petrus in navi. Johannes legit.

> Equoris unda ferit hunc ; ille silentia querit ;
> Sic requies orat dum mandi cura laborat.

4. Leah et Rachel cum Jacob.

> Lyah gerit curam carnis ; Rachel que figuram
> Mentis, cura gravis est haec, est altera suavis.

5. Jesus et Apostoli colligunt spicas. Mola fumus et Apostoli facientes panes.

> Quod terit alterna Mola lex vetus atque moderna
> Passio, crux Christi fermentans cibus iste.

Petrus et Paulus cum populis.

> Arguit iste reos, humiles alit hic Phariseos,
> Sic apice tritae panis sunt verbaque vitae.

6. Jesus cum Samaritana Synagoga et Moses cum quinque libris. Ecclesia de gentibus ad Johannem.

> Potum quesisti fidei cum Christe sitisti.
> E qua viri cui sex Synagoga librique sui sex,
> > delicta notat hydria fonte relicta.
> Ad te de gente Deus ecclesia veniente.

7. Samaritana adduxit populum ad Jesum. Rebecca dat potum servo Abraham. Jacob obviat Rachaeli.

> Fons servus minans pecus hydria virgo propinans
> Lex Christo gentes mulierque fide redolentes.
> Jacob lassatus Rachel obvia grex adaquatus
> Sunt Deus et turbe mulier quas duxit ab urbe.

FENESTRA SEXTA.

1. Jesus loquens cum Apostolis. Gentes audiunt. Pharisei contemnunt.

> Sollicitae gentes stant verba Dei sitientes
> Haec sunt verba Dei quae contemnant Pharisei.

2. Seminator et volucres Pharisei recedentes à Jesu. Pharisei tentantes Jesum.

> Semen rore carens expers rationis et arens
> Hii sunt qui credunt, tentantes sicque recedunt.
> Semen sermo Dei, via lex secus hanc Pharisei insidiator.
> Et tu Christi sator

3. Semen cecidit inter spinas. Divites hujus mundi, cum pecunia.

> Isti spinosi locupletes deliciosi
> Nil fructus referunt quoniam terrestria querunt.

4. Semen cecidit in terram bonam. Job. Daniel. Noah.
Verba prius servit Deus his fructus sibi crevit
In tellure bona, triplex sua cuique corona.

5. Jesus et mulier commiscens sata tria. Tres filii Noae
cum Ecclesia, Virgines, Continentes. Conjugati.

Parte, Noe nati, mihi quisque sua dominati,
Una fides natis ex his tribus est Deitatis.
Personae trinae tria sunt sata mista farinae
Fermentata sata tria tres fructus operata.

6. Piscatores. Hinc Pisces boni, inde mali. Isti in
vitam aeternam.

Hii qui jactantur in levam qui reprobantur
Pars sunt à Domino maledicta cremanda camino
Vase reservantur pisces quibus assimulantur
Hii quos addixit vitae Deus et benedixit.

7. Messes. Seges reponitur in horreum. Zizania in
ignem. Justi in vitam aeternam. Reprobi in ignem aeter.

Cum sudore sata messoris in horrea lata
Sunt hic vexati sed Christo glorificati.
Hic cremat ex messe quod inutile judicat esse
Sic pravos digne punit judex Deus igne.

8. De quinque panibus et duob. piscibus satiavit multa
millia hominum. D^{us} Sacerdos. Rex.

Hii panes legem, pisces dantem sacra Regem
Signant quassatos à plebe nec adnihilatos.

Synagoga cum Mose et libris Ecclesia cum Johanne.
Quae populos saturant panes piscesque figurant
Quod Testamenta duo nobis dant alimenta.

FENESTRA SEPTIMA.

1. Cvravit Jesus filiam viduae. Ecclesia de gentibus
cum Jesu. Petrus orat et animalia dimittuntur in linthea.

Natam cum curat matris prece ; matre figurat
Christo credentes primos, nataque sequentes.
Fide viventes signant animalia gentes ;
Quos mundat sacri submersio trina lavacri.

2. Curavit Jesus hominem ad piscinam. Moses cum
quinque libris. Baptizat Dominus.

> Lex tibi piscina concordat sunt quia quina
> Ostia piscinae, seu partes lex tibi quinae.
> Sanat ut aegrotum piscinae motio lotum
> Sic cruce signatos mundat baptisma renatos.

3. Transfigurationem Domini. Angeli vestiunt mortuos
resurgentes. Angeli adducunt justos ad Deum.

> Spes transformati capitis, spes vivificati
> Clares in indutis membris à morte solutis.
> Cum transformares te Christe, quid insinuares
> Veste decorati declarant clarificati.

4. Petrus piscatur et invenit staterem. Dominus ascendit
in Hier. Dominus crucifigitur.

> Hunc ascendente mox mortis adesse vidente
> Tempora ; te Christe piscis praenunciat iste
> Ludibrium turbae Deus est ejectus ab urbe.

5. Statuit Jesus parvulum in medio Discipulorum. Mo-
nachi lavant pedes pauperum. Reges inclinant doctrinae
Petri et Pauli.

> Hoc informantur exemplo qui monacliantur
> Ne dedignentur peregrinis si famulentur.
> Sic incurvati pueris sunt assimulati
> Reges cum gente Paulo Petroque docente.

6. Pastor reportat ovem. Christus pendet in cruce.
Christus spoliat inferna.

FENESTRA OCTAVA.

Dominus remittet debita servo poscenti.

> Ut prece submissa sunt huic commissa remissa
> Parcet poscenti seu parcit Deus egenti.

Petrus et Paulus absolvunt poenitentem et Dominus sibi
credentes. Servus percutit conservum. Faulus lapidatur.
Stephanus lapidatur.

Cur plus ignoscit Dominus minus ille poposcit
Conservum servus populus te Paule protervus
Regi conservo repetenti debita servo
Assimulare Deus Martyr nequam Phariseus.
Tradidit cum tortoribus. Mittuntur impii in ignem.
Judæi perimuntur.
Cæditur affligens, captivatur crucifigens
Hunc punit Dominus flagris, hos igne caminus.

FENESTRA NONA.

Homo quidam descendebat de Hier. in Jerico et incidit
in latrones.
Perforat hasta latus, occidit ad mala natus.
Creatur Adam. Formatur Eva, comedunt fructum,
ejiciuntur de Paradiso.
Ex Adae costa prodiit formata virago.
Ex Christi latere processit sancta propago.
Fructum decerpens mulier suadens mala serpens.
Immemor authoris vir perdit culmen honoris
Virgultum. fructus. mulier. vir. vipera. luctus
Plantatur. rapitur. dat. gustat. fallit. initur.
Poena reos tangit, vir sudat, foemina plangit.
Pectore portatur serpens, tellure ribatur.
Sacerdos et Levita vident vulneratum et pertranseunt.
Vulneribus plenum neuter miseratus egenum.
Moses et Aaron cum Pharaone. Scribitur tau. Educitur
populus. Adorat vitulum. Datur lex. Elevatur Serpens.
Pro populo Moyses coram Pharaone laborat
Exaugetque preces, signorum luce coronat,
Cui color est rubeus siccum mare transit Hebraeus.
Angelico ductu patet in medio via fluctu.
In ligno serpens positum notat in cruce Christŭ
Qui videt hunc vivit, vivet qui credit in istŭ
Cernens quod speciem Deitatis dum teret aurum
Frangit scripta tenens Moyses in pulvere taurŭ.

Samaritanus ducit vulneratum in stabulum cum jumento.
Ancilla accusat Petrum.　Dominus crucifigitur. sepelitur,
Resurgit.　Loquitur Angelus ad Marias.

Qui caput est nostrum capitur : qui regibus ostram
·Prebet, nudatur : qui solvit vincla ligatur.
In signo pendens.　In ligno brachia tendens.
In signo lignum superasti Christe malignum
Christum lege rei, livor condemnat Hebraei
Carne flagellatum, rapit, attrahit ante Pilatum
Solem justitiae tres, orto sole, Mariae
Quaerunt lugentes, ex ejus morte trementes.

FENESTRA DECIMA.

Suscitat Jesus puellam in Domo.　Abigael occurrit David
et mutat propositum.　Constantinus jacens et matres cum
pueris.

Quae jacet in cella surgens de morte puella
Signat peccatum meditantis corde creatum
Rex David arma gerit, dum Nabal perdere quaerit.
Obviat Abigael mulier David, arma refrenat.
Et nebulam vultus hilari sermone serenat.
Rex soboles Helenae, Romanae rector habenae
Vult mundare cutem quaerendo cruce salutem.
Nec scelus exerces, flet, humet, dictata coercet.

Dominus suscitat puerum extra portam.　Rex Solomon
adorat Idola et deflet peccatum.　Poenitentia Theophili.

Qui jacet in morte puer extra limina portae
De foris abstractum peccati denotat actum.
Errat foemineo Solomon deceptus amore :
Errorum redimit mens sancto tacta dolore
Dum lacrimando gemit Theophilus acta redemit
Invenies veniam dulcem rogando Mariam.

Dominus suscitat Lazarum.　Angelus alloquitur Jonam
sub hedera ante Ninevem.　Poenitentia Mariae Egiptisae.

Mens mala mors intus ; malus actus mors foris : usus
Tumba, puella, puer, Lazarus ista notant.

Pingitur hic Nineve jam pene peracta perire
Veste fidus Zosimas nudam tegit Mariam.
Mittit Dominus duos Discipul. propter asinam et Pullum.
Sp. sanctus in specie columbae inter Deum et homenum.
     Imperat adduci pullum cum matre Magister
     Paruit huic operae succinctus uterque minister,
     Signacius simplex quod sit dilectio duplex
     Ala Deum dextra fratrem docet ala sinistra.
Jesus stans inter Petrum et Paulum.
     Genti quae servit petris Petrum, petra mittit,
     Escas divinas Judeis Paule propinas.
Adducunt discipuli Asinum et Pullum.   Petrus adducit
ecclesiam de Judeis.   Paulus adducit ecclesiam de gentib.
     Quae duo solvuntur duo sunt animalia bruta
     Ducitur ad Christum pullas materque soluta.
     De populo fusco Petri sermone corusco
     Extrahit ecclesiam veram referando Sophiam
     Sic radio fidei caeci radiuntur Hebraei
     Per Pauli verba fructum sterilis dedit herba
     Dum plebs gentilis per eum fit mente fidelis
     Gentilis populus venit ad Christum quasi pullus.
Occurrunt pueri Domino sedenti super Asinam.
  Vestibus ornari patitur Salvator asellam
  Qui super astra sedet, nec habet frenum neq. sellam.
Isaias dicit.   Ecce Rex tuus sedens super asinam.
     Qui sedet in coelo ferri dignatur asello.
David ex ore infantum, etc.
     Sancti sanctorum laus ore sonat puerorum.

FENESTRA UNDECIMA.

In medio caena Domini David gestans se in manibus suis.
Manna fluit populo de coelo.
     Quid manibus David se gestans significavit
     Te manibus gestans das Christe tuis manifestans

Manna fluit saturans populum de plebe figurans
De mensâ Jesu dare se coenantibus esum.
Lavat Jesus pedes Apostolorum.   Abraham Angelorum
Laban camelorum.

Obsequio lavacri notat hospes in hospite sacri
Quos mundas sacro mundasti Christe lavacro
Cum Laban hos curat, typice te Christe figurat
Cura camelorum mandatum Discipulorum.

Proditio Jesu.   Venditio Joseph.   Joab osculatur Abner
et occidit.

Fraus Judae Christum, fraus fratrum vendidit istum
Hii Judae, Christi Joseph tu forma fuisti.
Foedera dum fingit Joab in funera stringit
Ferrum, Judaicum praesignans fœdus iniquum.

Vapulatio Jesu.   Job percussus ulcere.   Helizeus et
pueri irridentes.

Christi testatur plaga Job dum cruciatur
Ut sum Judeae, jocus pueris Helisee.

FENESTRA DUODECIMA.

Christus portat crucem.   Isaac ligna.   Mulier colligit
duo ligna.

Ligna puer gestat, crucis typum manifestat.
Fert crucis in signum duplex muliercula lignum.

Christus suspenditur de ligno.   Serpens aeneus elevatur
in columna : Vacca comburitur.

Mors est exanguis dum cernitur aereus anguis
Sic Deus in ligno nos salvat ab hoste maligno
Ut Moyses jussit vitulam rufam rogus ussit
Sic tua Christe caro crucis igne crematur amaro.

Dominus deponitur de ligno.   Abel occiditur.   Heliseus
expandit se super puerum.

Nos à morte Deus revocavit et hunc Heliseus
Signa Abel Christi pia funera funere tristi.

Moses scribit Thau in frontibus in porta de sanguine

agni. Dominus in sepulcro. Samson dormit cum amica
sua. Jonas in ventre ceti.

> Frontibus infixum Thau praecinuit crucifixum
> Ut Samson typice causa dormivit amicae.
> Ecclesiae causa Christi caro marmore clausa.
> Dum jacet absorptus Jonas Sol triplicat ortus,
> Sic Deus arctatur tumulo triduoque moratur.

Dominus ligans Diabolum. Spoliavit infernum. David
eripuit Oves et Samson tulit portas.

> Salvat ovem David : sic Christum significavit,
> Est Samson fortis qui rupit vincula mortis
> Instar Samsonis, frangit Deus ossa Leonis,
> Dum Sathana stravit, Chr^tus. Regul jugulavit.

Surgit Dominus de sepulcro. Jonas ejicitur de pisce.
David emissus per fenestram.

> Redditur ut salvus, quem ceti clauserat alvus :
> Sic redit illesus, à mortis carcere Jesus.
> Hinc abit illesus David : sic invida Jesus
> Agmina conturbat, ut victa morte resurgat.

Angelus alloquitur Mariam ad Sepulcrum. Joseph extrahitur è carcere. Et Leo suscitat filium.

> Ad vitam Christum Deus ut leo suscitat istum,
> Te signat Christe Joseph ; te mors ; locus iste.

STORIES.

The Forester whose Throat was Pierced Through.[1]

"Adam, a young man to whose care a certain nobleman
had entrusted the charge of his goods, having two companions
with him, caught three other men who had killed a deer (*lit.*,
a wild beast), and with the intention of assailing them as
thieves endeavoured to lay hands on them and take them.
But one of them casting a dart pierced the throat of his

---

[1] Will. I., p. 342.

assailant. And he, after taking a few steps, fell down, and, feeling the severity of the wound, cried : ' O Thomas, martyr, have mercy on me, lest I die of the wound I am suffering from, while through my careful stewardship thou art afraid of accepting my master's guarantee of payment.[1] I will go, as a pilgrim and devotee, to the house which thou hast stained with thy blood.' He said his prayer and drank the martyr's water ; but in order that the danger due to the place and manner of the wound might be made evident to the sufferer, whereby he might rise to praises the more devout from the favour of the divine bounty, the water began to run out from either side of his throat. Besides, whatever food or drink he took passed out on one of the two sides, so that many people, fearing for his life, declared that the arteries were injured, and we, so far as we could judge from the wound that was to be seen, suppose that the wound was in his throat. But the martyr, to whom the Lord of power had granted power, ordained that within three weeks' time he was cured at Canterbury."

THE WOUNDED CARPENTER.[2]

" A carpenter had made a vow to go to the scene of the martyrdom of the servant of God. The carpenter's name was William (of Kellett). And while he put off fulfilling his vow, on a certain day in the morning, after shutting up his house, he made the sign of the holy cross on his forehead, and commended himself to the protection of the saint Thomas. Coming, moreover, to the appointed place and applying himself to his work, he raised his axe, but since his hand erred in directing a blow on a log, the steel buried itself in his shin ; and, since the bone was cut, it (*i.e.*, the steel) sent forth marrow as well as blood. Sinking to the ground in a swoon, he was borne up and carried back home. Then to those who were present binding up the wound and

---

[1] Query.   [2] Will. I., p. 273.

preparing plasters he said : 'Let not mortal aid be sought. I commit the whole case to the Lord and to the martyr Thomas.' And falling into a trance he perceives the martyr speaking to him. 'It was a very good thing for you this morning to have remembered me, for unless I had held the handle (of your axe) you would have pierced right through your shin and would have lost it entirely. Now, indeed, power has been given me from the Lord to heal you.' Saying this, he raised his hand and made on him a sign of cure. The wounded man, roused at the voice of the speaker, broke forth into the words : 'Loose my leg. I am whole, the blessed Thomas has cured my wound.' And so it was found (when the bandage had been taken off) just as he said ; the wound was healed, the leg thus suddenly restored whole with medicine, having no sign of the wound, except the mark of a very light scar. Hence this is made evident because the vows are performed which are rightly vowed to the Lord ; for it is better not to make a vow than not to fulfil a vow when it is made."

ROBERT OF CRICKLADE, PRIOR OF S. FRIDESWIDE'S, RELATES HIS RECOVERY.[1]

"About twelve years ago or more, when I was in Sicily and was intending to go from the State of Catania to Syracuse, I was walking beside the Adriatic Sea ; for so my path ran. A southerly gale and the surf of the sea, which was on my left, gave me a swelling of my foot and skin with a very bad inflammation. But the next day but one, which I spent at Syracuse, I applied fomentations and plasters and got better, and when I got back to Rome I cured myself still more perfectly by medicine, and had no more trouble during my return to England. But during the last three or four years, as I calculate, the illness has attacked me so violently that I have not been able to allay the disease by

[1] Bened. II., p. 97.

draughts or blood-lettings (in spite of using numbers of
leeches) nor by plasters or fomentations or ointments. At
last two abscesses burst on my foot, so that I could not put
on or draw off my boot without great pain. Why say
more? I understood that the disease was chronic, and not
to be cured by hand of man ; for doctors say : 'Chronic
diseases die with you'. The people of our country are my
witnesses, for when I used to address them on feast days,
urging them to the best of my ability to follow the path of
righteousness, even at times when clergy from different
places in England were present, I used to excuse myself
from standing on account of the above-mentioned pain, and
to address them sitting. Last Lent I was being consumed
with grief because I could not take part in the divine
celebrations as had been my wont, and specially at the
thought of the mystery of our Lord's Passion, the yearly
occurrence of which was close at hand. For I was afraid I
should not be able to celebrate it as was my duty, and I kept
praying in my heart to the Lord to turn His face from my
sins and hear me, so that on those days at least I might be
enabled by His favour to do what belonged to my office.
And He in whose hand is health granted me this favour,
unworthy as I am, that from the day of the Last Supper up
to the fourth festival in Easter (? week) my pain was so far
abated that, to the astonishment of myself and my brethren,
who knew my disease, I performed all my duties in accordance
with my prayer, after which the pain returned. Now I had
it in my mind that the $\left\{ \begin{array}{l} \text{signs} \\ \text{wonders} \end{array} \right\}$ of the most blessed
Martyr are $\left\{ \begin{array}{l} \text{said to happen} \\ \text{to be heard of} \end{array} \right\}$ at his tomb. But when I
had come to Canterbury, through the length of the journey
and the strain of the effort the disease became worse, the
swelling increasing. Lying, however, before his tomb I
prayed the Lord to save me through the merits of His
martyr from my sickness, and I prayed the martyr to plead

with the Lord for me.   Then, ignorant that my prayer was heard, I returned to the hostelry heavy-hearted and groaning, because I knew not how I could ever return to my own home on account of the excessive pain.   At last the thought occurred to me to anoint my foot with the holy water which had been given me ; and placing my foot in a basin, I made the sign of the cross with the water on my foot and shin in the name of the Holy Trinity and in memory of the most blessed martyr, and anointed both.   I had the remainder thrown into the fire, that it might not be trodden under my feet.   On the morrow, as I was journeying homewards to my own country, I felt the pain abated and an easement of the swelling ; but when I was in my hostelry at Rochester, wishing to see the easement I felt, I could espy nothing.   I again anointed myself in the same way.   The next day, going to London, I felt the pain still more relieved and a greater easement of the swelling, and when I took off my boot in London I clearly saw that this was the case.   And when I had reached Oxford, having finished so much of my journey . . . I now found myself completely cured. . . . I add this much, that I can bear every strain of walking or standing on that shin and on that foot quite as well as— indeed (I feel) better—than on the other foot which was not affected."

This account, as set down here at our request, the above-mentioned prior wrote in all haste about himself, desiring to recount his story rather than to show his literary ability.

The Two Lame Damsels.[1]

" Two damsels, the daughters of Godbold of Boxley, who from their very cradles had supported themselves on crutches rather than on their feet, were brought thither.   While they were both imploring the martyr to heal them, a sleep fell upon the elder.   In her sleep the saint comes and addresses

[1] Bened. II., p. 170.

her, and both promises health and grants it. On waking she finds with surprise her hamstrings lengthened to the accompaniment of a great dance of clergy and laymen. Meanwhile the banners of the church are shaken,[1] and she is led into the church. This the younger sister sees, and gives way to more violent tears, as much sadder for her own ill fortune as her elder sister is overjoyed by her good. She blames the saint because while her sister has departed she is left prostrate. You could see there the lamentation of Esau, who cried aloud for the gift of his father's blessing : ' Hast thou not one blessing for me, O my father? Bless me, me also, I beseech thee ! ' And as she wept with bitter cries, the holy father was moved within him and came to her next day as she slept and restored her to health like her elder sister. Thus the miracle was twofold, and double glory is given to God and double rejoicing to men."

A Boy upon whom a Wall Fell.[2]

" A boy named Godfrey, a native of Winchester, son of a certain Robert and Lettice, when he was about sixteen months old, was very sick of a fever, but on drinking the water of S. Thomas he cooled down and rejoiced the hearts of his parents. But their sudden joy was overclouded by sorrow, for while his mother was sitting at home some way off from him, the wall of the house fell with a shock from top to bottom, and the child was asleep in his cradle underneath. The wall was of stone, thirteen feet high. And so the cradle, which was made of solid planks four-square like a carved box, was broken into eight or ten pieces, and some of the fragments were buried deep in the ground. It was thought that the wall fell on account of a storm the day before, but we believe that this was brought about for the glory of the sainted Saint of Saints. But the mother, seeing that her little one was buried in the ruins, cried out : ' S.

---

[1] Query.   [2] Will. I., p. 206.

Thomas, save the child that thou gavest back to me!' and
for sorrow shrieked and fell in a faint.   O marvellous kind-
ness of the Saint!   O marvellous power of the unconquered
Martyr, who both listened without a moment's delay to the
pious mother and saved the boy beyond all desert of his,
unharmed in the jaws of death, while three or four cartloads
were heaped upon him.   For when on one side the boy was
overwhelmed in the ruins, and on the other the mother in
sorrow, two men came in, and raising the woman to her feet,
asked and learned the reason of her grief.   Then, after
summoning help, they pulled away the mass of ruins and
found the cradle broken to bits, but lift up the boy not only
unbruised but happy and laughing, 'tis marvel to tell, not
having a trace of a bruise on his whole body, except a slight
blackening of one of his eyes that could hardly be seen.   As
time went on, and those who were assisted by the grace of
the martyr were giving thanks, the boy began to fall sick
and to be prayed for in the due course of public intercession.[1]
And it happened on a day that a certain woman went to the
child's grandmother and came in and said : ' It has been
revealed to me concerning the child that he ought to be
taken to the memorial of the blessed Thomas.   Know that
this revelation has come from the Lord.   For I do not say
this for the sake of gain or for any other less honourable
reason, but I am here as the messenger of God's warning.'
And so after a little time the boy was taken to Canterbury,
and we learnt this story."

The Workman who was Buried Alive.[2]

" Thomas the martyr, by a new kind of miracle, gave a
lesson of brotherly love and ecclesiastical peace to his rival,
Roger, Bishop of York, a man most highly learned in things
human and divine, had he been wise in accordance with his
wisdom.   Roger, when priest, brought a supply of water

---

[1] Doubtful.   [2] Will. I., p. 253.

(? siquidem) to his village of Churchdown from the brow of
a hill about 500 yards away.　But there is a rising ground
halfway, looking down with head erect upon the flats of the
surrounding fields, about twenty-four feet high.　When the
work was in full swing this was cut through so as to receive
the aqueduct in its open breast and give it a straight passage
through.　In charge of the work was one William, who had
hired his workmen from the neighbouring town of Gloucester.
As he was fixing a leaden pipe at the bottom of the cutting
in the hill, a fallen mass of the excavated earth came down
upon him.　His fellow-workmen sprang apart in all direc-
tions, and when they were hoping to dig him out, covered
round as he already was, lo! there was another landslip and
a crumbling and overhanging mass slipped down and caught
the young man.　The landslip could be estimated at about a
hundred cartloads.　There he stood, on his back, with his
hands spread out before his face, clad in nothing but his
shirt, as he had been working hard.　And seeing that all
escape was cut off, he turned his hopes to the Lord, the first
and last refuge in every case of need, and also invoked the
blessed Virgin Mary, who, as her name shows, is the star to
the haven of eternal happiness for men tossed in the stormy
sea of human misfortunes.　But the Lord did not help at
the invocation of His name, because He was about to glorify
His martyr.　What can the wretched man do, caught by so
great a downfall? . . . He begins to be swollen with
choking breath, and while tortured in the effort to breathe
out there comes to his lips the name of Thomas the martyr.
(He prays.)　All this happened in the heart of the earth.
But there arose a cry: 'A priest, a priest, because he is
dead!'　The priest was summoned, performed the funeral
service, and when it was finished, returned to his own
business. . . . The Lord became his helper in this sore
plight.　For a woman of the place had a dream, and said to
her son in the early morning: 'I think, my son, that the
buried man is still alive, for I saw in my sleep that he was·

both drinking milk and sleeping on it '. Forthwith, contrary to his wont, her son rose from his bed and went out into the fields, not on purpose, but as chance led him ; and, as if guided by the Spirit, he came to the place, not of the water's flow, but of the water's woe, and putting his ear to the ground he heard as it were a groan. He called to the watchman of the fields, who had gone out in the morning to see to the herd which he had turned into the open air at night, and said : ' Ho there ! he is still alive, for I hear as it were the dismal groan of a man '. The other answered : ' There is nothing there, and I would not believe there was, though every one in Gloucester swore to it '. ' Come and listen,' said the first. And when they had done so, the other told the priest that the man was alive, and forthwith the priest broke off divine service and came with the people to the place. And news was sent to Gloucester in the same way that the man was still breathing. And all holy and humble men of heart came thither, old men, boys and women, and began with diligence to dig out the earth with brooms, dishes, buckets and other country tools. But the buried man, hearing them making a stir and taking each other's places at the work, began to call up from below to the bystanders near and far not to hurt him with their picks, and not to work too far off ; and the day advanced to the third hour. Then at last the buried man was brought to light, with his cheeks crushed together and his arms bruised but not actually broken, and all stiff and numbed with the keen frost underground. And so he was brought back to the upper world that sinners might escape from the nether."

MODERN WINDOWS.

Under the south-west Tower in the Nave is a memorial window to Sir R. H. Inglis by the late Mr. G. Austin. On the north and south sides of the Nave are four Te Deum windows by the late Mr. George Austin. Under the north-west

Tower are memorial windows to Mrs. H. Austin and to Mr. George Austin, architect and surveyor of the Cathedral, who died in 1848. He was the father of Mr. George Austin, who designed and gave the stained glass windows in the Clerestory of the Nave, and to whom reference is made in connection with the modern windows. Mr. Harry Austin, architect and surveyor of the Cathedral, who died in 1892, was his brother.

On the north side of the Nave is a memorial window to Dean Stanley, presented by Messrs. Clayton & Bell. In the four lights are figures of Archbishops Odo, Stigand, Lanfranc, and Prior Eruulf, and beneath are scenes in the history of the Cathedral.

In S. Michael's Chapel the window on the south side is also by Messrs. Clayton & Bell, with figures in the four lights of S. Gregory, S. Augustine, Ethelbert, and Bertha, and scenes connected with their history beneath. The east window is by Messrs. O'Connor of Birmingham. The west window in the Martyrdom is by Messrs. Ward & Hughes. It was given by the late Rev. R. Moore.

In the north-east Choir Transept is a memorial window to Lord Kingsdown by Messrs. Clayton & Bell. On the north wall are two by Messrs. Powell. The one to the west was given by Mrs. Robertson in memory of her husband, Canon Robertson. The figures are those of Abel, Enoch, Noah and Shem ; and Abram, Melchizedek, Isaac and Jacob in the adjoining window.

Beneath is one in memory of Canon Chesshyre by Messrs. Hardman, and another by Mr. G. Austin. In the adjoining Chapels are two more by him. A memorial window in S. Martin's to Dr. Spry,[1] and in that of S. Stephen, one presented by Dean Stanley.

In the north aisle of the Choir there is a memorial window to Archbishop Howley by Mr. G. Austin, and the

---

[1] An old medallion is preserved here—S. Martin dividing his cloak with the beggar.

Triforium windows above, and also on the south side, are by him, in memory of the Dean and Mrs. Lyall.

In the Trinity Chapel is a memorial window to Lieut. R. G. Dyson, 3rd Dragoon Guards, by Messrs. Clayton & Bell.

In Becket's Crown is a window by Mr. G. Austin, and in the south aisle of the Choir is another in memory of Canon Lockwood. Three windows in the south side are by Mr. Wailes.

In S. Anselm's Chapel all the windows are by Messrs. Clayton & Bell, and presented by Canon Holland, by whom the Chapel was restored. In the east window is a figure of S. John.

In the apse is one with figures of SS. Peter and Paul, to whom the Chapel is dedicated.

The five lights of the window on the south wall contain figures of Stephen Langton, the Black Prince, S. Anselm, the Fair Maid of Kent and Archbishop Theodore.

On the west another window represents Archbishops Mepham and Bradwardine, who are buried in the Chapel.

On the south side of the east Transept of Choir are two small windows and two large by Messrs. Clayton & Bell, the large one to the east in memory of Dean Alford, the other to Mr. E. Leigh Pemberton. On the west is another in memory of the Marquis Conygham also by them. To the east are two windows by Mr. G. Austin.

For EU product safety concerns, contact us at Calle de José Abascal, 56–1°,
28003 Madrid, Spain or eugpsr@cambridge.org.

* 9 7 8 1 1 0 8 0 1 1 3 3 4 *